To Eric, Sam, Justine, Philip,
Hannah and Isabelle

LOUISA BLAIR

The Anglos

The Hidden Face of Quebec City

VOLUME II
Since 1850

Library and Archives Canada Cataloguing in Publication

Blair, Louisa

    The Anglos: the hidden face of Quebec City / Louisa Blair.

    (La bibliothèque de la capitale nationale)
    Co-published by: Commission de la capitale nationale du Québec.
    Contents: v. 1. 1608–1850 – v. 2. Since 1850.
    ISBN 2-921703-57-2 (v. 1). – ISBN 2-921703-59-9 (v. 2)

1. Canadians, English-speaking – Québec (Province) – Québec – History.   2. Québec (Québec) – History.   I. Commission de la capitale nationale du Québec   II. Title.   III. Series.

FC2946.9.E55B53 2005   971.4'471   C2005-901419-9

LOUISA BLAIR

The Anglos

The Hidden Face of Quebec City

VOLUME II
Since 1850

This publication was made possible thanks to an initiative
by the Commission de la capitale nationale du Québec.

Commission de la capitale nationale

Publishing Director: Denis Angers
Project Coordinator: Hélène Jean
Historian: Nicolas Giroux
Archivist: Éric Turcotte

Éditions Sylvain Harvey

Publisher: Sylvain Harvey

Picture research: Jacques Saint-Pierre

Documentary research: Lorraine O'Donnell, Jean-Philippe Garneau

Editing: Robert Chodos

Graphic design: Interscript

Printing: Transcontinental

The publishers wish to thank the following partners for their
contribution to the marketing of this book:

Literary and Historical Society of Quebec
CBC Quebec Community Network
Quebec Chronicle-Telegraph

Front cover: *Quebec from the River St. Lawrence*, James Busick Hance,
ca. 1903 (detail).

Inside front cover: *Quebec City from Sillery Hill*,
Miriam P. Blair, 1999.

Inside back cover: *Plains of Abraham*, Miriam P. Blair, 1999.

First edition, 2005
© Commission de la capitale nationale du Québec
and Éditions Sylvain Harvey
ISBN 2-921703-59-9

Printed in Canada

Legal deposit – Bibliothèque nationale du Québec, 2005
Legal deposit – Library and Archives Canada, 2005

Éditions Sylvain Harvey
Phone: (418) 692-1336 (Quebec City area)
Toll-free: 1 800 476-2068 (Canada and U.S.A.)
E-mail: info@editionssylvainharvey.com
Website: www.editionssylvainharvey.com

Commission de la capitale nationale du Québec
Phone: (418) 528-0773
Toll-free: 1 800 442-0773
E-mail: commission@capitale.gouv.qc.ca
Website: www.capitale.gouv.qc.ca

Distribution in bookstores in Canada

Distribution Ulysse
Phone: (514) 843-9882, extension 2232
Toll-free: 1 800 748-9171
E-mail: info@ulysse.ca

Éditions Sylvain Harvey wishes to acknowledge the contribution of the
Société de développement des entreprises culturelles du Québec
(SODEC) to the publication and promotion of this book.

Government of Quebec – Tax credit for book publishing –
Administered by SODEC

This book is also available in French under the title:
LES ANGLOS : La face cachée de Québec, Tome II, Depuis 1850
ISBN: 2-921703-60-2

Acknowledgements

Thanks above all to my partner Don Hembroff and daughter Miriam for their support and tolerance of my absence-even-when-present; and to my beloved extended family.

With the paucity of published sources, and a deadline that made delving into archives impossible, I relied heavily on oral interviews for this period of anglophone history in Quebec City. For this volume I would therefore like to thank all interviewers and interviewees, especially Lorraine O'Donnell, Karen Kawawada, Mary Ellen Reisner and Marianna O'Gallagher; also Koula Aaron, Jennifer Alexander, Athanase Athanassiou, Hugh Bignell, Eric Blair, Justine Blair, Ronald Blair, Frank Cannon, Rita Devlin, Marc Drolet, James Donovan, Patrick Donovan, Scott Emery, Louise Escojido, Jules Goodman, Max Gros-Louis, Joanne Hardy, Jack Harlow, Deborah Hook, Diane Kameen, Lupita Kerwin, Tess Leblanc, Brian Lee, Pavel de Liamchin, George Lovett, Mary McGreevy, Patrick McKenna, Karen Macdonald, David Mendel, Clive Meredith, Diana Meredith, Tom Moore, Bill Ray, Regina Rosenhek, Prachi Shah, Kathleen Stavert, George Thomson, Brian Treggett, Peter Vaughan, Aline Visser, Richard Walling, Jan Warnke, Bruce Willett, Kuo Goun Woo, Napoleon Woo, Jane Wong, and, last of all, the late Dr. Larkin Kerwin, whom I was privileged to interview shortly before his death in 2004.

For the pictures I would like in addition to thank Jacques Saint-Pierre, Miriam Blair, Barbara (O'Halloran) Bignell, Bill Noonan, Timothy Stavert, Yves Beauregard, Mike Reshitnyk, Frédéric Smith, Simon Carmichael and Rita Marsh.

Thanks also to Diana Apedaile, Dennis Apedaile, Peter Dunn, Tim Earle, Jan Earle, Helen Meredith, Edward Murphy, France Parent and the ever-helpful and long-suffering staff of the Literary and Historical Society of Quebec.

Preface

In Europe, history is very *old*, and in Quebec City we take pride in the fact that we have some of that Olde Worlde character here too. But much of the history I relate in this second volume, covering the period from 1850 to the present day, is young enough to live vividly in the bodies and minds of the people. Questions are asked; stories are told. Recipes, songs, jokes, traditions, family traits and languages spoken are passed down, and history lives.

One of my Blair ancestors went to work for Quebec City timber merchant William Price in the Saguenay in 1842. A century later, my father still worked for Price Brothers, which sent him to England to sell newsprint to the British press barons. Hence my British upbringing. Hence also my interest in journalism – my family's history in Quebec has left its stamp on my life.

But although family stories and personal destinies may tell us something of the history of Quebec City anglophones, little of this more recent history has been written down. The interest of historians in anglophone Quebecers was deflected at Confederation, and by the 1940s had almost vanished completely. The few books that cover the period are mostly personal memories or local and particular histories, *la petite histoire* as we say in French. Records are buried, statistics ungathered, archives scattered across the country. So without apology I refer often to my grandmother's family, the Marshes, who have given me a glimpse into the vicissitudes of one anglophone middle-class late Victorian Quebec City household. I also relied heavily on more than 50 interviews.

Combing through documents looking for anglophone names and skipping over francophone ones was an often uncomfortable, at times unwholesome and ultimately misleading experience. So while I hope that this volume might provoke further research, and partially unveil the hidden face, I also hope we soon put this history back on track as an integral part of the whole.

Louisa Blair

Table of contents

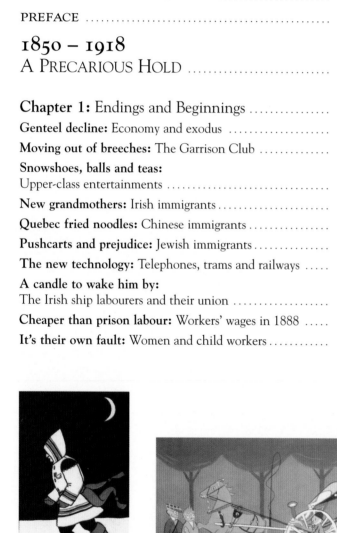

We cannot forget that we stand here today as members of the greatest Empire of the world – yes, the mightiest Empire the world has ever seen.

– Henry Roe, Anglican Archdeacon of Quebec,
Sermon preached for the Queen's Jubilee, 1887

1850 – 1918

A precarious hold

Quebec City anglophones in the second half of the nineteenth century began to hear new sounds, see new faces, and dream new dreams.

The tramp of marching feet faded when the British soldiers of the garrison went home. The frantic flap of dozens of sails being hoisted was heard less frequently down in the port: steamships were taking over. The scurrying feet of civil servants were stilled when the city lost its status as Canada's capital. The humming of trains and trams on metal tracks and the hiss and whirr of engines gradually replaced horseshoes striking on cobbles and the squeak of cartwheels. From across the sea an imperial summons sounded, and in the streets Chinese and Yiddish mingled with French and English.

In this period a long struggle to determine identity and allegiances expressed itself through law, language and religion. While francophones looked to Rome and the Catholic Church, the anglophone elites looked to London and the British Empire. Churches both Catholic and Protestant were booming, sometimes at each other, and creating new societies and institutions such as the Jeffery Hale Hospital and St. Brigid's Home. Irish immigration contributed a grandmother to many francophone Quebecers, and Irish ship labourers formed an effective union. But the timber and ship-building trades were being replaced by industrial manufacturing. Women and children worked in the new factories too – for a pittance.

Chapter 1

Endings and Beginnings

While the anglophone gentry with their snowshoe clubs, skating parties and afternoon teas behaved as if nothing was amiss, their numbers were in decline and the economy was undergoing a sea change. Irish, Jewish, American and Chinese immigration was shifting the composition of the city's English-speaking population and, with the advent of industrialization, apprenticeship gave way to wage labour. Poverty-stricken ship labourers finally organized to challenge the status quo of boss-worker relations.

The Skating Carnival, Arthur Elliot, 1881.
By flooding the floor of an old warehouse
on Quai de la Reine in the 1850s, anglophone
Quebecers built one of North America's earliest
indoor skating rinks. At the Quebec Skating
Rink, built in 1877 across Grande Allée from
the Parliament buildings, elegant masked balls
at Mardi Gras shared the ice with rough hockey
matches. In 1899, according to local lore, Arthur
Smith of the Quebec Hockey Club invented
the goal net. Quebec City hockey players won
the Stanley Cup in 1904, and in 1911–12
the Quebec Bulldogs won the championship
of the world.

Genteel decline

Economy and exodus

By the end of the nineteenth century Quebec's timber trade was exhausted. Duties on Baltic timber had long been abolished, as were most duties on trade with the United States in 1854. Sawn lumber was now being shipped from Montreal and the Ottawa Valley via the new canals and railways which, thanks to the efforts of Montreal entrepreneurs, avoided Quebec City. As railway links with the east were restricted to the south shore until the completion of the Quebec Bridge in 1917, some Quebec City merchants moved across the river and set up their businesses in Lévis. Shipbuilding, too, began to decline as the British were busy building cheaper steel ships.

Everybody blamed everybody else for Quebec City's decline. The government blamed the merchants for not investing in the new steel-hulled ships and the railways. The merchants blamed the government for not investing in the shipyards and the port. As for the decline in the timber trade, they also blamed the new labour organizing among bargemen, shipsmiths and the Quebec Ship Laborers' Benevolent Society, which was at last forcing an end to some of the most inhumane labour practices. The banks didn't care who was to blame. Many whose headquarters were in Quebec City, such as the Quebec Bank and the Union Bank of Lower Canada, upped sticks and moved to Montreal.

The garrison was also to leave during this period (1871), depriving the city of several hundred rowdy British soldiers, many illegitimate births, the active participation of the officers in the city's clubs, sports, theatre and musical events, and lucrative contracts in bread, salt pork, rum and showshoes. English speakers dropped from 40% of the population in 1851 to 30% in 1871.

Ethnic rivalries in this period of economic uncertainty sometimes became violent. In the 1872 federal election, James Gibb Ross ran in Quebec Centre against Joseph-Édouard Cauchon, one of the city's most prominent francophone politicians. The culmination of a bitter election campaign fought along ethnic lines was a pistol fight in the Protestant Cemetery on Rue Saint-Jean, in which many rioters in both camps were injured and one of Ross's supporters, David Gandle, was shot and killed. Cauchon beat Ross by 330 votes, and some disappointed anglophones wrote to the papers saying they were leaving Quebec.

By 1901 the anglophone population was down to 15% of the city's population. While the numbers of anglophones declined, many of the old merchant families remained. The Prices moved from the timber business into pulp and paper in the Lake St. John (Lac Saint-Jean) and Saguenay regions, while the Breakeys concentrated on the Chaudière region and the Atkinsons on the Etchemin. The Rosses continued to flourish, as did the Davie family, who controlled the only large surviving shipyards. The English-speaking community was now largely autonomous, and even the English they spoke was closer to that of the British Isles than to that of Ontario.

60ᵗʰ Regiment leaving the Citadel, Quebec, *L'Opinion publique*, 1871.

After Quebec had lived through a century of real or imagined threats of invasion by the Americans, the British finally signed a peace treaty with them in 1871. Six months later, to the dismay of the Canadian government which didn't relish having to raise its own troops, 3,000 British soldiers and their retinue marched out of the Citadel for the last time, paraded in full regalia down to the Lower Town singing "Auld Lang Syne" and caught their ship back to England. That day anglophone Quebec City was deprived of both a pack of trouble on payday and prestigious matches for its daughters.

The steamer *Spartan*, anonymous, ca. 1870.

Steam-powered passenger vessels were the height of modernity. By 1825 the Lachine Canal enabled them go up beyond Montreal without being towed by oxen; they were later aided by new navigational equipment such as gas-fired buoys and steam foghorns. But coming downriver again from Kingston, the wilderness still won out: to the delight of W.G. Anglin, a Scottish traveller aboard the *Spartan* in 1876, steamers still ran the rapids, "drawing from the passengers exclamations of wonder and delight. Before shooting the Lachine rapids we took on board the Indian pilot, Baptiste Delisle, a noble looking fellow with an eye like an eagle's."

Quebec Snow Shoe Club

SEASON 1913-1914.

Quebec Snow Shoe Club, 1913–1914.

The anglophone gentry continued to amuse themselves by dressing up in blanket coats (Quebec clubs sported a red stripe) and literally running across country on snowshoes. "Gray-haired men leap fences like boys," wrote an astonished visitor, "while others attempt a race with a locomotive. The horses on the road are frightened by their shouts, but the snowshoers are lost to everything but their own pleasure." The Roman Catholic Church disapproved of snowshoeing, with the women dressed indecently in trousers. It warned people sternly against all manner of clubs, as well as circuses, novels, theatres and modern dances such as the waltz and the polka.

Moving out of breeches

The Garrison Club

"Down to the Victorian age, men drank to get drunk," wrote historian William Wood, "and it was considered an insult to the host if you went away sober." He recalled black barmen in Quebec who used to inquire, "Drink sir? Drinky for drunky or drinky for dry?" Earlier in the century, the Baron's Club, whose members met at the Union Hotel on Place d'Armes, could happily spend 250 guineas on a single evening's entertainment, leaving at 4 am. Not everyone lasted that long, however. "A few went home," wrote Wood. "Others were taken home. Others were on the floor. But some remained victorious, and occasionally able to dance the dinner out in triumph on top of the table."

No one observing the drinking habits of Quebec City's gentry would have guessed that anyone was worried about the economy. For wealthy men who wanted to simply get drunk and horse around together, however, the extravagance of the Baron's Club was replaced by the slightly more reasonable Stadacona Club in 1861, founded by city notables, half francophone and half anglophone. This in turn was succeeded by the Garrison Club, made up first of officers and later opened to civilians. It merged with the Cercle universitaire in 1984 and became known in French as the Cercle du garnison. Now 93% of its 800 members are francophone. It is housed in a British army building dating back to 1820 on St. Louis Street, just inside the city gates.

In the early days of the Garrison Club hard drinking was still a venerable tradition in Quebec City. One of the club's first concerns was that its private shipment of wines and spirits from Britain had been mistakenly redirected to Portland, Maine. Winter had set in, and the errant ship could not simply sail on up the coast, so arrangements were made to transport the shipment in a special stove-heated railway wagon to Quebec City. In addition to their concern for their spirits, members were also much preoccupied with honour and reputation. One member was expelled for failing to take legal action to quash malicious rumours that were circulating about him. Rats were also circulating maliciously, chewing the furniture and house linen to shreds, and in 1892 the club purchased a scotch terrier to quash them.

In 1864 members were allowed for the first time to wear pants, instead of breeches. But women did not darken the front doors of the Garrison Club until 1981, when Cabinet Minister Lise Payette refused to enter through the side door. As a club historian wrote the year before, "Needless to say the marks of deference and courtesy which ladies in mixed company demanded from gentlemen were inconsistent with the pursuit and enjoyment of good 'fellowship.'" He added sullenly, "No law ever prevented women from forming their own clubs." The first Jew was admitted to the club in 1972.

French and English speakers socialized together, but "le Chambre des Anglais," known to the "Anglais" themselves as the Wheel House, was where English only was spoken, while French was spoken in "le Chambre des Canadiens." On New Year's Day the doors between these two rooms were thrown open and the two peoples, so to speak, kissed and made up. While French is now the majority language spoken at the Garrison Club, there is still a lively coterie of English speakers who meet at the Wheel House on a weekly basis, sitting around the perimeter of the room under the gaze of the portraits of the governors general and, according to a time-honoured tradition, taking their lunch on trays.

At the Garrison Club and other clubs of the *moyenne bourgeoisie*, social mingling between French- and English-speakers was the norm. In contrast to Montreal, which was still in the grip of a small number of immensely wealthy English speakers, in Quebec City the two groups got on reasonably well. They met around bank boardroom tables to deal with financial matters, or at the Quebec Harbour Commission and the Quebec Chamber of Commerce. They collaborated keenly on such projects as union breaking, arguing against any form of accident compensation, and complaining together to the government that those troublesome Irish ship labourers were bringing down Quebec City's timber business.

Snowshoes, balls and teas

Upper-class entertainments

While older anglophones were meeting at the Garrison Club, Quebec City's young blades were taking boisterous delight in the outrageously long and cold winters. They joined the Aurora, the Waverley, the Emerald or one of the many other snowshoe clubs, as well as the Driving Club or the Tandem Club. Four-in-hands were considered the most "aristo" of all and, according to William Wood, "The two star turns were to go clear into and out of the Ursulines Lane [Ruelle des Ursulines] without a check, and to trot full pace down Sillery Hill [Côte de l'Église], sharp curves and all." Snowshoe clubbers went out for bracing all-day hikes, ending up at a tavern or a clubhouse and singing songs they composed themselves. Snowshoe races on the Esplanade or on the river were "the most popular event of the winter life," wrote a journalist in *Harper's Magazine* in 1888: "The Saint Louis Road is filled with fine equipages set off with rich furs; the sidewalks, the high snow-covered city walls, and the glacis are diversified with stamping and stirring crowds." In 1898 snowshoers were sufficiently athletic and numerous to be seen forming a human triumphal arch over the roadway at the winter carnival procession.

It was by joining one of the snowshoe clubs that Cornelius Krieghoff, an impecunious artist from Holland, inserted himself into upper-crust Upper Town society in 1851. After "bilking" the city's tollgates (racing through without paying), Krieghoff and his friends usually topped off a day's wild riding or sleighing with a visit to Ambroise Gendron's Inn near Montmorency Falls, which they transformed into "a bedlam of dancing, whooping, horse-play and buffoonery." Krieghoff held his drink much better than the other "roisterers," so when the rest of the crowd was too drunk to sing and the musicians too drunk to play, he jumped up on the stage, grabbed a violin, and played better than most of the hired musicians. Then he went home and painted one of the very sights he had just seen or escapades he had partaken in, selling the results to his delighted friends. Other keen customers were Quebec City's increasing numbers of tourists, and British officers wishing to take home a souvenir of their sojourn in Quebec City.

Krieghoff was one of the first artists to depict rural French Canadians, and his romantic and admiring depictions of the *habitants*, or the noble Indian standing under a lone oak tree looking out across the river, went down well in both England and New England. In his 700 paintings he replayed the same themes over and over, as most struggling artists do, and he added to his income by teaching art to young ladies at Mrs. Browne's Academy on St. Ursula Street (Rue Sainte-Ursule), which involved teaching them to copy his own paintings down to the tiniest detail.

Portrait of Krieghoff, J.E. Livernois, ca. 1870.

According to his closest friend in Quebec City, John Budden, Cornelius Krieghoff wasn't just a brilliant artist; he was also "a capital musician and understood [music] in all its branches, used to play and compose music for hours every day. He had a most wonderful faculty for picking up languages, spoke and wrote English, French, Italian, Spanish, German and Dutch, Latin and Greek; was deep in Natural History." Another friend, Christopher O'Connor, said that listening to Krieghoff talk "was more like reading well written books" than listening to ordinary conversation.

Breaking Up of a Country Ball in Canada, Early Morning, Cornelius Krieghoff, 1857.
Krieghoff based this picture on Ambroise Gendron's Inn, near Montmorency Falls, in which he and his bourgeois anglophone friends held rowdy all-night parties. The innkeeper hands back a violin to a departing musician, a snowshoer fills his pipe and revellers continue carousing on the gallery while a passing sleigh on the way to market overturns, tipping its passengers into the snow, including a large pig.

Once their daughters were of the marrying age, wealthy families such as the Prices, Breakeys and Powers threw debutante balls at the Château Frontenac to mark the young ladies' "coming out." An orchestra was hired for the evening and dancing went on until the early hours of the morning. These occasions enabled matches to be made between families who considered each other to be of the right social standing, both anglophone and francophone. A smart uniform on a man, however, could make up for lack of breeding.

Social life among the women of the elite was a continuous round of "trousseau teas" and "at-homes." Four anglophone neighbourhoods took turns having at-homes. On Fridays it was the Cape's turn (Saint-Denis, Sainte-Geneviève, d'Auteuil, Sainte-Ursule); on Saturdays the Ramparts; Grande Allée and Rue Saint-Louis on Thursdays; and from de Salaberry to Maple Avenue on Wednesdays. If the hostess was absent, each guest placed a calling card with her name on it on a silver tray by the door. If there had been a death in the family, the calling card was rimmed with black. When the hostess was "at home," the cook sent up trays of silver teapots and jugs, porcelain teacups and plates of biscuits, cakes and muffins from the kitchen, which was always in the basement. If the maid was lucky, the house had a miniature elevator or dumbwaiter for this purpose. Tea was then served in the living room by the maid in a little white apron.

Tobogganing on the Glacis, John B. Wilkinson, ca. 1870.

Sliding was not just a game for children. It was a stolen opportunity
for young men and women to clasp each other tightly as they lost control
on Quebec City's steep hills. In 1894 Mary Ann Glass wrote breathlessly
in her diary that "Charlie Billingsley was sliding with Edith down Bishop's
Hill & not being familiar with the sharp turns he went over a flight of steps.
Fortunately she rolled off at the top but he went all the way down and
was considerably stunned."

**Quebec Seen from the Pointe Levy,
Cornelius Krieghoff, 1853.**

This was a popular view of Quebec, and
Krieghoff published two versions in the same
year, as well as several prints. In line with the
romantic and picturesque tastes of anglophone
gentry, he also painted every waterfall within
visiting range of the city. Krieghoff was no social
reformer, however, and studiously ignored
the scenes of poverty in Saint-Roch on the way
to Montmorency Falls. When he wasn't painting
or composing, Krieghoff went curling, ice-
boating on the river, horse racing on the Plains,
tobogganing on the Glacis, sleighing or moose
hunting. In the evening he rehearsed with
his friends at the Histrionics theatre club.

Life into my bones

Hunting expeditions

Boys of the bourgeoisie were initiated young into the hunting and fishing life. In the summer of 1858, the president of the Quebec Game Club, Colonel William Rhodes, took his sons out to the woods to learn the ropes with the Huron. "We camped out for ten days and enjoyed our Indian life ...; one of the boys Godfrey is only eight years of age, but he is as active as a squirrel in the woods and we caught plenty of fish, I and the children were well amused. Boys make good hunters, they eat and sleep well." Legend recounts that Rhodes killed four caribou with a single shot in 1865. On returning from a month's hunting trip, Rhodes wrote to his uncle, "I like a good hunt. It does put such life into my bones. I can walk all that is old out of my frame in no time, and it is a great consolation to bully the Doctors instead of being at their mercy." Quebec historian James MacPherson Le Moine recounts that Rhodes was seen entering town with a dozen sleighs, topped with antlers, followed by another two full of hare, grouse and ptarmigan. The last sleigh contained a wolverine plus the colonel himself, "who seemed to be determined to kill every animal in the country."

A *Tenting Party*,
Alicia Killaly, ca. 1860.

New grandmothers

Irish immigrants

The maid who carried the silver trays and tea services up and down the stairs from the basement was, as often as not, Irish.

In 1851 nearly 4% of Ireland's total population emigrated, and almost every family had a leg over the Atlantic. Although Irish immigration to Quebec City slowed down to only 5% to 10% of the total by the late 1850s, by 1861 the Irish were nearly one third of the city's population. They were young, willing to do any work and, while Ontario was teeming with Protestant Orangemen, Catholics were welcome in Quebec. Irishmen already dominated the police force and public works, and readily hired their own countrymen. There was still plenty of work loading ships, too.

Officials at Quebec City tried to keep immigrants travelling west, however. As the timber trade declined, many of the men did move on to the United States (it was cheaper to come to Canada and then travel south overland than to take a ship straight to New York), or farther west to work on the newly developing canals, railways and, later, roads. Between 1871 and 1901 the Irish population of Quebec City declined by half.

Many young women stayed in Quebec City and worked as dressmakers, boarding-house keepers and domestic servants, and later in the factories that were beginning to replace the old port industries. Irish servants traditionally worked for a few years in domestic service before marrying. Because of the paucity of Irish men (in 1861 two thirds of the Irish between 15 and 24 years old were female) and the churches' disapproval of interfaith marriages, many Irish women married Catholic francophones, undeterred by the shouts of "pea soup!" and "patte-à-poil!" ("hairy legs!") that anglophones and francophones traditionally hurled at each other. Many Irish orphans of Black '47 were also assimilated into French-Canadian society. The saying goes that every Quebecer has an Irish grandmother, but it is difficult to identify Irish women who married francophone men after 1871. Their maiden names disappeared from the census once they married.

When work for ship labourers dried up in the 1880s and Irishmen departed for Montreal and elsewhere, skilled British industrial workers began to immigrate in greater numbers. By 1891 more British Protestants were arriving than Irish Catholics.

"Aux places d'eau, les derniers préparatifs," *Le Monde illustré*, 1900.

Servants preparing the household for the move to a summer residence. As the 19th century wore on and the Victorian equation of cleanliness with godliness took hold, life became even harder for the servants: yet more water to be hauled up and down the stairs, and more laundry. Fashionably late dining meant they got less sleep. Homemaking was now graced with the title "domestic science," and servants had to undergo rigorous training that went into fierce detail about their duties. Many young women opted to work in the new factories instead, where there was more freedom and less isolation.

Quebec fried noodles

Chinese immigrants

A long way culturally and economically from the Irish working in the ports and the basement kitchens of the Cape were the Chinese, who began arriving in Quebec City late in the nineteenth century. They opened hand laundries in St. Roch, taking people's washing into their own homes, ironing and starching for a small fee. By 1902 there were 30 laundries in the city.

Early arrivals lived on Côte d'Abraham before settling in the Chinatown below the cliff. Many were members of the Chi Kung Tong, a secret political society dedicated to restoring the Ming Empire. Most Chinese joined the revolutionary Kuomintang, whose headquarters, under the name Chinese Nationalist Party, is still at 617 Rue Saint-Vallier.

When the Kuomintang took power in China in 1911, *Le Soleil* reported that several Chinese men went to Mr. Bouchard, the barber on Rue Saint-Jean, to have their braids cut off, required by the new Chinese government as a sign of loyalty. When Quebec City's Chinatown was largely destroyed by the hubristic highway building of the 1960s, the remains of the Chinese community moved farther down Rue Saint-Vallier or out to Charlesbourg.

The papers warned people not to frequent Chinese laundries because they were dirty, and *Le Soleil* complained that the Chinese used their laundries simply to "amass piastres which then enable them to go and live like pashas in China." Incidents were reported of Chinese being beaten up in their laundries or restaurants, and sometimes a crowd would join in. In spite of this aggression, the Chinese adapted to life in the new country by learning English and French and inventing their own Quebec-Chinese recipes such as "Quebec Fried Noodles." They also kept their old traditions alive, celebrating Chinese New Year and the festival of respect for the dead, Ching Ming, well into the 1960s. They opened businesses with other Chinese families, something rare in China, and the folk tales they chose to pass on to their children were the legends that spoke of mutual respect and toleration. They had to stick together to survive.

Chinese laundry, 126 Rue du Pont.

In the early 20th century, Irish servants were able to hand over laundry duty to the poorest of the new immigrants, the Chinese. Mr. Kuo Gon Woo was 16 when he started working in his grandfather's laundry: "Work started at 4 am, when someone had to light the coal burner to get the water boiling in the tanks, light another in a huge drying room full of washing lines, and another to heat up the irons in the ironing room. My bed was one of the ironing tables. There were four of us sleeping in one room, and we cooked and ate there too."

Group of Chinese in front of the Nationalist League on Côte d'Abraham.

The Chinese had to stick together, as they suffered racist attacks in Quebec City. "Two Chinese who run a laundry on St. Joseph Street were attacked after dark ...," reported *Le Soleil* in August 1903. "The Chinese tried to force the attackers off the premises. Passersby, seeing what was going on, entered the laundry and started beating the Chinese." Legislation barred all Chinese immigrants from 1923 to 1947, including the wives and children of those already here. The women shown here are the wives of visiting Chinese delegates. Fred Wong (Chinese name: Wong Thuey Way) wasn't able to bring his wife Yet Lang and their two children from China until 20 years after he immigrated.

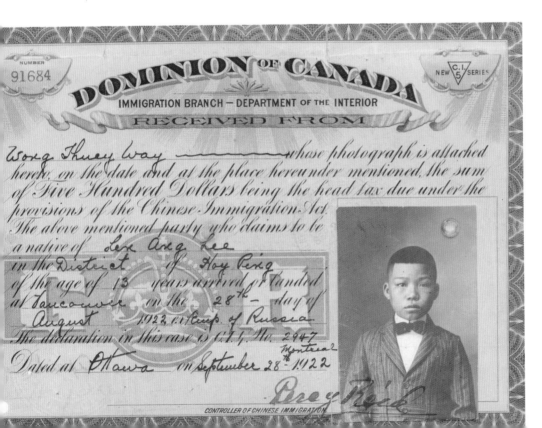

Fred Wong's head tax, 1922.

As soon as the Canadian Pacific Railway was completed, the federal government began to restrict Chinese immigration by imposing a head tax on immigrants. It was increased to $500 in 1903 – the equivalent of two years' wages for a Chinese labourer at the time. Fred Wong's head tax was paid by a family friend. "When he was a boy he couldn't go to school because he was working in a laundry," said his daughter Jane, "but he went to Sunday school at Chalmers Church. That's where he learned English. It opened doors for him, and he sent all his children to Quebec High School."

Pushcarts and prejudice

Jewish immigrants

Although there had been Jewish traders and merchants in Quebec since the eighteenth century, a new wave of Jewish refugees fleeing from pogroms in eastern Europe began to arrive in the early 1880s. These Romanian, Austrian, Polish and Russian Jews had little in common with resident Jews such as the Joseph, Hart and Franks families, some of whom had already been in Quebec for seven generations. By 1910 Quebec City's Jewish population had increased from a handful to almost 400.

Many of the Jewish immigrants began their lives in Quebec City as pedlars, walking or driving their carts from house to house to sell wares. The fortunes of some rose quickly, such as Maurice Pollack, the great Quebec City retailer and benefactor. Others fit into the business world less easily. Jewish Quebecer Rachel Smiley remembered:

> My father had to leave Romania because he was one of the few educated Jewish people there. Somehow he had managed to get permission to study the Romanian language. Jewish business people were taxed much higher than anybody else, and they objected. My father drew up the petition. After that he was warned that he'd better leave and he left that same night.
>
> He wasn't much of a salesman, but he did what everybody else did in Quebec, carried a pack on his back and tried to sell things. He was an intensely religious man. He carried his Talmud with him and he was forever studying that. He wouldn't eat meat or bread, because it wasn't kosher. So he suffered hunger pains and took pain killers, which were considered the cure-all for everything. They burned up his intestines. He wasn't the kind of man who made fortunes. He was here for five years before he was able to send for his family.

Jews settled in the Saint-Jean, Saint-Louis and Saint-Pierre districts, and specialized in trade and industry, especially clothing manufacture. While the Jewish retail stores on St. Joseph Street are remembered by many Quebecers, there were also Jewish doctors, administrators, lawyers, accountants and civil servants. They sent their children to the Protestant English schools, which had opted to also educate children who were neither Protestant nor Catholic.

David Goodman and Israel Shoel Rosenhek, pedlars, ca. 1895.

David Goodman and Israel Rosenhek came from Austria around 1895. Local businesses wouldn't give Jews jobs, so they peddled with a horse and cart until they could open their own stores on St. Joseph Street. Goodman and Rosenhek travelled around buying furs from farmers and trappers to sell to Montreal furriers. On the road they slept in barns, or if they were lucky, with a Jewish family. Quebecer Regina (Vinegar) Rosenhek said, "We were the only Jews in our village. In winter the Jewish pedlars all stopped at our place. In the morning I could smell their coats and socks drying over the potbellied stove."

Russian Jewish immigrants arriving in Quebec, William James Topley, ca. 1911.

Beginning in 1881, tens of thousands of eastern European Jews such as this Russian family fled pogroms and sought new homes in Canada. But to immigration officials' dismay, the Jews did not fit their stereotype of the ideal immigrants, "stalwart peasants in sheepskin coats" who would farm, mine or chop trees. They settled in the cities. Maurice Pollack, who became a well-known millionaire and philanthropist, arrived in Quebec from Russia in 1902 at the age of 17, and opened his clothes shop on St. Joseph Street in 1906.

Ultramontane rage

The Ortenberg-Plamondon case

In Quebec the new influx of Jews coincided with a wave of Catholic Ultramontanism. Among other things, Ultramontanists believed that the Catholic Church's main enemy was a powerful Judeo-Masonic conspiracy that controlled the press. "The Jews," wrote Jules-Paul Tardivel, "are a curse, a curse from God." In 1910, after relentless pulpit attacks on local Jews by one priest, the city council put a tax on Jewish pedlars, hoping to limit the number of Jewish settlers in the town. Successful Jewish merchants were often the scapegoats for resentment towards the less visible anglophone bosses, while the English-speaking elite were anti-Semitic in their own more distant way, such as excluding Jews from membership in the Garrison Club. Neither the race-based nationalism of French speakers nor the "binational" consensus that was at its height at the turn of the century included Jews.

When the Jewish socialist Freemason mayor of Rome, Ernesto Nathan, dared to criticize the pope for interference in Italian politics, the Ultramontanists of Quebec were outraged. A demonstration in Montreal in 1910 attracted 25,000, and Quebec City, not to be outdone, held its own demonstration a week later. The Montreal Yiddish paper, the *Keneder Odler*, reported that Quebec City's was "much worse and much much blacker ... the local Jews are very frightened and have remained in their homes, fearing to go out lest they be attacked." In May 1910, the journalist J. Édouard Plamondon spoke to a Catholic youth organization rally, accusing the Jews of vicious crimes, including ritual murder. Some participants vowed to boycott Jewish merchants, and then a crowd went down to St. Joseph Street and broke the windows of local Jewish homes and businesses, harassing an old Jew on the street on the way. One of the Jewish merchants whose property was damaged, Benjamin Ortenberg, took Plamondon to court for Jewish losses resulting from his speech, and won the case on appeal.

St. Joseph Street, Valentine & Sons Publishing Co., ca. 1910

The new technology

Telephones, trams and railways

It was a young Jewish Pole called Sigismund Mohr who introduced the first telephone company to Quebec City.

Canada's first long-distance telephone conversation had taken place between Mr. Watson in Quebec City and Mr. Badger at the Montreal Fire Alarm Telegraph Company in 1877. The same year, Mohr demonstrated the city's first telephone line between Lavigne's store and the priests' recreation room at the Séminaire de Québec. Soon there were two telephone companies in competition in the city, so that for a while people had to have two telephones, one for each system.

Mohr's most impressive feat, though, was installing 34 electric lights on Dufferin Terrace in 1885, powered by the Montmorency Falls. Twenty thousand people were there to applaud as they lit up "as if by a magic wand." Soon electricity was all the rage, and the city is now so lit up that birds, unable to navigate by the stars any more, get lost and die.

It was the "eccentric and clever" Scot, James George, who had come up with the idea back in the 1820s of transporting people in trams pulled by horses. Everyone laughed at him. His other suggestion, that someone should work on making the St. Lawrence River navigable upstream from Montreal, had met with a similar reaction. Samuel Hough instituted public transport in 1845 when he started the horse-drawn Cap Rouge Omnibus, which carried passengers from downtown to Cap Rouge and back three times a day. But the first tram did not appear in Quebec City until 1865, 40 years after James George's brainwave. It was pulled along St. Paul, St. Joseph and St. Vallier streets by a pair of very tired horses.

Horse-drawn tram at the Champlain Market.

The first "street railways" were installed in Quebec in 1863 by the Quebec Street Railway Company and used cars pulled by horses. The tramline ran from Champlain Market to St. Sauveur along St. Paul, St. Joseph and St. Vallier streets. The St. John Street Railway (1870) ran along Buade Street, down La Fabrique and St. John Street to the old Sainte-Foy tollgate. In winter the floors were strewn with straw in lieu of heating, and the conductor marched up and down beating his arms to keep from freezing. By 1897 electricity had been invented, so the exhausted horses returned to their stables.

Tramlines didn't help matters for pedestrians, cyclists or the new motor-cars, the first of which was driven down Sainte-Foy Road at 29 kilometres per hour in 1897. At the end of the nineteenth century even the macadamized roads of Quebec City were still huge mud puddles for five months of the year. While the Lower Town foundered in mud, major arteries were asphalted, and in 1886 Grande Allée was paved with slices of red pine set in concrete.

Many pioneers of the new transportation technologies were of American, British or Irish origin. The children of the timber merchants and the shipbuilders entered the fray with their customary gusto, particularly once railways, with large quantities of money at stake, became the rage. The family of Irish shipbuilder Thomas Hamilton Oliver demonstrated this tendency: his grandson worked for the Lake St. John Railway Company and his great-grandson for the Canadian National Railways.

In 1869 an American railway contractor named J.B. Hulbert had the extraordinary idea of building a railway out of wood. Amid a storm of excitement, maple rails were laid running south about 40 kilometres to Gosford. They only lasted three years, but that was long enough to infect the people of Quebec City with "railway fever," which almost bankrupted the city (it spent a million dollars) and the province (it spent $12.5 million), and brought down several governments. Premier Henri Gustave Joly de Lotbinière, the first president of the Quebec and Gosford Railway Company and an inveterate train fiend, made numerous noble attempts to raise money for railways, including collecting from house to house in his snowshoes. When railways had nearly emptied the provincial treasury he proposed abolishing the Legislative Council to save money.

The Lake St. John Railway created a northern hinterland for the city, and American tycoons built hunting and fishing camps up and down the length of the track, expropriating the land from the Huron. They hired them as guides, but punished them if they continued to hunt and trap on their ancestral lands. The most ambitious of the new railway projects was the North Shore Railway between Quebec City and Montreal, first proposed in the 1850s and, after several bankruptcies and reorganizations, finally completed under government ownership in 1879. It tied Quebec City and the north shore communities into the growing Canadian economy, but was not enough to prevent the emergence of Montreal as the leading railway hub and the province's most important city.

Private enterprise still had the bit firmly between its teeth during this period, as typified by the proudly monopolistic Quebec Railway, Light and Power Company, which hoped to run pretty well everything in town. Its success was eventually to contribute to Quebec nationalists such as René Lévesque saying, "Enough, you greedy people! The State will run everything now!" – and ushering in Hydro-Quebec (see chapter 4).

Quebec City's favourite mode of transportation of all, the *funiculaire*, was built by W.A.G. Griffith in 1880 at a cost of $30,000. Like other early commuters, Dorothy Marsh used to take "the terrace elevator," as she called it, to the Lower Town in the early twentieth century to her job in the Quebec Bank, where her father, a shoe manufacturer, was a director. A 20,000-litre tank teetered at the top of the cliff and a 40,000-litre tank at the bottom, and the elevator was powered by a 9-kilowatt steam pump that moved these vast weights of water. The ubiquitous Quebec Railway, Light and Power Company, not to be outdone, opened another *funiculaire* in 1901 to take tourists up to the top of the Montmorency Falls.

The Quebec Bridge, Central Span, **Henry Ivan Neilson, 1916.**
Quebec City's isolation from pan-Canadian trade was broken with the opening of the world's longest cantilever bridge in 1917. Although it was the pride of many British schoolboys, who earnestly learned its dimensions by heart, it was a bridge of many sorrows, falling into the river twice before its completion and taking 88 workers, 33 of them Mohawks from Kahnawake, to their deaths. The Phoenix Bridge Company paid $1,800 to the widow and seven children of Harry French in compensation, and $450 to the parents of 14-year-old bridge worker Stanley Wilson. It never attempted any grand-scale projects again.

Workers on railway at Portneuf.
The Anglican Church sent missionaries to the Transcontinental Railway camps in 1908. Rev. G.R. Fothergill, visiting the Quebec section of the railway, found English-speaking workers who were Anglican, Roman Catholic, Presbyterian, Lutheran, Baptist and Methodist. The men slept in log shacks on two broad shelves, two or three to a bunk. "The work on the grade is hard ...," he reported, "filling trucks with earth and sand or dragging stones to build up the dump ... working with a pick and shovel in the cuts ... – and some of the men have become rough, too."

Give the steamboats away

Horace Jansen Beemer

One of the "railway barons" of this era in Quebec City was Horace Jansen Beemer, the son of a Pennsylvania farmer, a man of astonishing energy who began his Quebec City career building parts of the Dufferin Terrace and the Kent and St. Louis gates during the mayoralty of Robert Chambers in the late 1870s.

By 1882 the Upper Town had paved roads, running water and pretty pseudo-Gothic turrets. But the St. Roch and Jacques Cartier districts still had no running water, so Horace J. Beemer set about providing the city with 75-centimetre water mains. Unfortunately, his pipes began to leak in a matter of hours. To field the angry calls, he and the waterworks engineer Jeremiah Gallagher had some of the earliest telephones in Quebec City installed in their houses. Another Irish-Quebec engineer, J.P. Connelly, was hired to install one-metre pipes specially imported from Scotland. They ran from Lake St. Charles all the way downtown underneath a street called l'Aqueduc. At last the town water was clean, but these pipes leaked too. By 1888 most of the town had running water, but the poorest still had to buy water at 10 cents per barrel and make do with outdoor privies.

Not to be discouraged by leaky pipes and overflowing toilets, Beemer made connections with the wealthy old Scots families of Frank Ross and Benjamin Scott and the Quebec Bank. Over the next several years Beemer built about a dozen railways, including those that opened up the Lac Saint-Jean region. His financial connections sometimes bore him up, sometimes let him down. When he built the Alexandra Bridge linking Hull and Ottawa, he had to mortgage his own house. He built a sawmill, several steamboats and two hotels in Lac Saint-Jean, to which he attracted many rich American salmon fishermen, including John D. Rockefeller. But alas, he was kicked off the board of directors of the Quebec Railway, Light and Power Company in 1899, his hotel in Roberval burned down, he gave his steamboats away, and in 1910 he died of exhaustion.

Horace Jansen Beemer, William Notman, 1881.

A candle to wake him by

The Irish ship labourers and their union

On the wharves at the foot of the *funiculaire*, the men who loaded the ships with timber were getting restive with their low wages and dangerous working conditions. Those building the ships, mostly French Canadians, Scots and English, were making double what the mostly Irish ship labourers made. They were so poor that if one of them became ill, his family fell quickly into destitution, and when he died, the workers had to pass around a hat to collect enough money for a coffin and a candle with which to hold a wake. Stevedore Thomas Cullen would later tell the Royal Commission on the Relations of Capital and Labor:

> Those were the days of poverty and oppression for the ship labourers … They were looked upon as nothing … After they would leave on Saturday night they would have to go to the stevedore's house in the hope of getting their pay, very likely a man would meet his wife on the way with her bonnet and shawl on, and the two of them would wait out in the cold for the stevedore in the hope of getting sufficient pay to keep his wife and family in food for the following week. They would wait, and wait, and wait, and often would see no stevedore and get no money … These men … were kept waiting out in the sleet and snow, or rain, for the stevedore's wife would consider her house too good to accommodate ship labourers.

In 1862 they formed the Quebec Ship Laborers' Benevolent Society, the most powerful union in nineteenth-century Canada. They held long hot outdoor discussions on Champlain Street on summer nights about the best way to negotiate. Members paid 24 cents a month to belong, and soon they had the courage to publish a list of the different jobs they had to perform and what they were worth. The *holders* had the dangerous job of receiving and stowing giant squared timbers in the hold of the ships. The *swingers* brought the logs over to the ship from the coves and spent

Loading ship with square timber through the bow port, Quebec, William Notman, 1872.

After the 1879 riots, a bylaw was passed requiring the hiring of both Irish and French-Canadian labourers. Foremen cannily put francophones on one side of the ship and anglophones on the other, so that competition to fill the holds was ferocious. Rogue logs killed or maimed many workers in the rush before winter closed the river, when many Irishmen migrated south to work through the winter in Louisiana, Alabama, Georgia and the Carolinas.

their lives waist-deep in water and chilled to the bone. They had to retire early, wracked with arthritis. Workers refused to work with the new steam-driven winches, which had killed several men because they were so noisy that if a man was pinned in the hold, no one heard him yell.

The list of requirements set off a huge ruckus amongst the ships' captains and the merchants who owned the operations, the St. Peter Street oligarchy that included Messrs Sharples, Ross, Wilson and Jeffery. The timber merchants quickly moved all their loading operations over to Lévis, on the far shore of the river, where union membership was weaker. The workers crossed the river one day and had the nerve to jostle Mr. Davie, owner of the Davie Shipyard (still a household name in Quebec City), in their eagerness to beat up the scabs who were working for him. The shipmasters finally agreed to the list in a historic meeting in Noonan's Imperial Hotel, forcing the merchants to capitulate too. By that time the ship labourers had been three weeks without pay.

Every July 23, the date of the founding of the Quebec Ship Laborers' Benevolent Society, the 2,000 members marched 13 kilometres through the streets of Quebec City holding a banner bearing the motto "We support our infirm, we bury our dead", stopping only to sing "Auld Lang Syne" or "The Rising of the Moon" outside the houses of well-wishers.

Les Émeutes de Québec, L'Opinion publique, 1879.

Ship labourers worked 11 hours a day at the dangerous and underpaid job of bringing timber from the coves and loading the ships. In 1879 the French-Canadian ship labourers' Union Canadienne published wages that were half those demanded by the Irish union, the Quebec Ship Laborers' Benevolent Society. Wearing top hats, the French Canadians marched defiantly down to Little Champlain Street, where the Irish longshoremen considered the wharves their exclusive domain and chased out French-Canadian intruders. The Irish set up barricades and a cannon in defence, and threw stones from Dufferin Terrace. Two men died and 30 were injured.

Cheaper than prison labour

Workers' wages in 1888

The timber industry continued to call for reform, by which it meant the outlawing of such unions. By that time, however, new industries had already started to take its place. The new bosses were only too happy to take up the slack and hire cheap Irish labour. Leather work and shoe factories began to fill the Lower Town.

By 1900 there were 225 tanneries and 9,000 workers in the tanning business alone, and Quebec City was the largest producer of shoes in the country. There were fortunes to be made. William Marsh, the son of Baptist minister David Marsh, started off as a humble shoe retailer on Couillard Street but ended up with the largest shoe factory in the city, employing 550 people who turned out 500,000 pairs of shoes per year. Paying the men, women and children piecework averaging $3 or $4 per week in 1888, ten years

later he was able to build himself a large mansion on Grande Allée, now the Vieille Maison du Spaghetti. A Toronto prison warden complained that Quebec City was producing shoes more cheaply than his inmates could.

Conditions were not much better for other workers around town. Firemen were on duty for 24 hours and had to snatch a few hours' sleep in the stables with the horses. Bakers in Quebec City had to work 14 hours, overnight, for $3 to $4 a week. James MacDermott, a carter (or "hackman"), made no more than $2 per day. The girls who worked in Mary Buchanan's laundry were paid 50 cents a day, and the stablemen who tended the tram horses for the Quebec Street Railway worked from 4 am to 11 pm for $5 per week, and had to sign an affidavit saying they wouldn't drink.

Some families earned so little money that they had to share lodgings, where a whole family might live in each room. John Hearn, the biggest landlord in Quebec City, admitted that the workers lived in very poor conditions, and that in the Champlain District sometimes six or seven houses shared one privy (an outdoor toilet consisting of a hole in the ground). In the winter when he went to collect the rents from his tenants, "In many instances they cannot

Wm. A. Marsh & Co. Ltd, shoe manufacturers, 472 Saint-Vallier, ca. 1912.
Quebec City had became the foremost shoe producer in Canada, and by 1915 William Marsh's shoe factory at the corner of Crown Street (de la Couronne) and Saint-Vallier was the largest in town. Marsh was an active member of the Protestant establishment, deeply involved in the Baptist Church, the YMCA and the Jeffery Hale Hospital. He spent most evenings either at the factory or at prayer meetings, leaving his wife at home with their nine children. On winter weekends he took parties of factory hands down in his sleighs to visit Montmorency Falls.

pay, and those who have to deal with them recognize the truth of this, and know that it is better not to trouble them." He blithely concluded, however, that "the city is very healthy, and the citizens enjoy good health, and live as long as most people." Meanwhile the toilets continued to overflow, there was still no public garbage collection, and two thirds of all reported deaths were of children under 15. As late as 1927, Quebec City's infant mortality rate was 147 per 1,000 live births. The only areas in the world with a higher rate in 2005 were sub-Saharan Africa and Afghanistan.

Sous-le-Cap Street, Henry Ivan Neilson, 1911.

When Isabella Bird travelled to Quebec from England in 1856, she was shocked by the poverty she found in the Lower Town: "Here are narrow alleys, with high, black-looking, stone houses, with broken windows pasted over with paper in the lower stories, and stuffed with rags in the upper … A little further are the lumber yards and wharfs, and mud and sawdust, and dealers in old nails and rags and bones … Here are old barrel-hoops and patches of old sails, and dead bushes and dead dogs, and odd saucepans, and little plots of ground where cabbages and pumpkins drag on a pained existence."

It's their own fault

Women and child workers

By 1871 women were 26% of the working population. Most were domestic servants, but about 1,800 women were already working in the new factories, many of them Irish immigrants who took their seats at the sewing machines beside increasing numbers of French-Canadian women. Children worked too, and employers sometimes hired whole families at a time.

Children in factories were fined for misbehaviour, and were in danger of getting caught in the machinery. The Royal Commission on the Relations of Capital and Labor of 1888 spent some time questioning staff at the Government Cartridge Factory on Cove Fields. They asked about the McLean boy, who came home at the end of the week with four cents' pay, and about some other children who were fined five cents each for playing during their dinner hour. They also asked questions about a little girl who lost part of her hand in the machine that she was operating. Thomas Lane, a machinist at the factory, testified that there were children as young as seven years old working there, while William Dickson, the foreman fresh from England, explained that children got injured because they didn't behave themselves. "They have no business underneath the machines," he said. "If a boy has to work a machine, he has no business to go this side or that side or get underneath it."

Child labour was no change from the preindustrial age, but in the past a child would have emerged from an apprenticeship with a well-learned trade. In the new factories, the employer simply got cheap labour, and the child acquired no knowledge that could improve his or her prospects. Legislation in 1885 kept women and children from working for more than 60 hours per week, and in 1907 the Public Assistance Act forbade children under 14 to work.

Women took little part in the labour movement, as the germs of a female workers' union were quickly swallowed up when the Catholic Church established its distinctly patriarchal unions.

Women working in arsenal, Quebec City.

Once the British troops had left for Britain, Canada began to train its own forces and produce its own munitions, including a federal cartridge factory which opened on Côte du Palais in 1882. The cartridges were tested in tunnels dug under the city, so that inhabitants could hear gunfire coming from below their feet all day long. Numerous accidents led to a new plant on Cove Fields, at the foot of the Citadel. Women were considered excellent workers in munitions, as they were patient and adept, and only earned half the wages of men. Children were paid 15 cents a day, and were fined if they misbehaved.

Very few of these women workers are likely to have heard renowned British suffragette Emmeline Pankhurst when she spoke for women's suffrage at Morrin College in 1916. By 1917 all the provinces west of Quebec had introduced suffrage, but it wasn't to arrive in Quebec for another generation. In his newspaper *Le Devoir*, Henri Bourassa wrote that it would destroy French-Canadian family values, hierarchy, authority and, in brief, society itself.

Alcohol, on the other hand, was not considered socially destructive enough to provoke serious prohibition in Quebec, in contrast to the other provinces. In 1919 Sir Lomer Gouin, Premier of Quebec, forbade the sale of liquor except for the purposes of industry, the church, medicine and "the arts." This rather fuzzy situation ended two years later when the *Loi des liqueurs* brought in state control that prevails to this day. Women in Quebec could not yet vote, but we could legally drink ourselves into oblivion.

Emmeline Pankhurst arrested by Superintendent Rolfe, London, May 1914.

In 1916 British suffragette Emmeline Pankhurst came to speak at Morrin College. She had been imprisoned in London for her militant activities in favour of the vote for women. During the war she half buried the hatchet, but couldn't resist expressing the hope that Quebec City women would launch their own suffrage movement. "If you are a human being you are entitled to the rights of a human being," she said. The next day the *Action Catholique* took exception: "Are not works of charity and Christian benevolence the proper role for woman, her particular privilege?" Quebec women could not vote in provincial elections until 1940.

Chapter 2

The Fashion for Institutions

*Q*uebec City's embrace of the nineteenth-century fashion for housing misfits in institutions continued well into the twentieth century. During this period anglophones vied with each other in building new asylums, orphanages and hospitals, such as St. Brigid's Home and the Jeffery Hale Hospital. Many were financed by wealthy male and female benefactors, and also by the churches, which were growing and multiplying apace. The St. Patrick's soirées and the Literary and Historical Society reached for the stars. The churches were heavily involved in education, and when the British North America Act enshrined separate education for Catholics and Protestants, each dug themselves separate trenches that lasted for well over a century.

Winter Sunset, from the Glacis,
James Busick Hance, ca. 1903.

To Europeans and Americans, Quebec was one of the most interesting regions of Canada. Many artists came to Quebec to paint, including Cornelius Krieghoff (Holland), Albert Bierstadt (Germany), Winslow Homer and John James Audubon (U.S.). James B. Hance (U.K.) attempted to capture that unique yellow light of a Quebec winter day. "Some there are, undoubtedly, who will fail to understand the color scheme of this picture," wrote a contemporary, "but to them I would say: Go to the Terrace some bright March afternoon just at sunset, and my word for it you will discover for yourselves how wonderfully Mr. Hance has caught the mood of that few moments."

Execution as entertainment

Quebec City's last public hanging

In the latter part of the nineteenth century, reformers and idealists began to notice that institutions did not cure all ills. Older institutions such as the Marine Hospital, the Beauport Asylum and the Quebec Jail were becoming dilapidated and overcrowded. In 1851 the Marine Hospital was so mired in filth and scandal that a royal commission was sent to investigate. In 1867 the last prisoner was moved out of the stinking and overcrowded old prison on Jail Hill (Chaussée des Écossais) to a new one on the Plains. And in 1884, the Beauport Asylum was reported to be a disgrace, with patients living in ill-ventilated cages.

The general public, moreover, was taking its own sweet time absorbing the enlightened ideals of respectful and humane treatment for all. The mad and the condemned were still considered excellent entertainment.

In 1864 the last public hanging in Quebec City took place in front of the Quebec Jail (later Morrin College). Public hangings were popular spectacles, but considered by the churches to be deeply unedifying. Bishop Baillargeon had a letter read from every Catholic pulpit forbidding the faithful to attend, but there was standing room only in the courtyard in front of the jail at 10 am on March 22, and later kneeling room only. Hundreds had come to watch John Meehan, an Irishman of 23, hang for murdering Patrick Pearl. Before being hoisted onto the scaffold by the "finishers of the law" in their black gowns and cowls, Meehan made a 15-minute speech in French and English, telling young people to stay away from bad company, drink, hatred and revenge. At the moment of his execution the crowd, including Baptist minister David Marsh's three-year-old daughter and the family maid, "uttered a deep prolonged moan or sob," fell on its knees, and prayed that John Meehan would now appear before his Creator. The Marshes' maid paid for this bad-taste outing with her job. You can still see the window at Morrin College from which unfortunate young men were "hanged by the neck 'til they be dead."

The Jail on St. Stanislas Street,
James P. Cockburn, ca. 1830.

The last resort of female Irish immigrants was prostitution, and Quebec's solution to prostitution was prison. In the 1850s, 80% of the residents of the women's wing of the prison on Jail Hill were Irish. A sign over the door of the prison (now the Morrin Centre) proclaimed, "May this prison teach the wicked for the edification of the good." While some took a lively interest in watching people hang, the Quebec Jail Association attempted the moral improvement of the prisoners.

Damnation as entertainment

Churches proliferate

Although the anglophone population of Quebec City was in decline, Protestant churches were proliferating. This had to do partly with the radical evangelical ideas coming over from Britain, partly with the fact that they had no pope to tell them what to do, and partly with the influence of the American circuit riders, itinerant preachers who rode through the countryside preaching colourful sermons about the inflammatory nature of hell and damnation. While some of the Protestant churches earlier in the century were refreshingly ecumenical, others had divided and sub-divided like hydra, writing vituperative tracts about one another's mistaken doctrines.

Some Presbyterians had split into the Free Church of Scotland, and built themselves an enormous church at the top of St. Ursula Street, still functioning today as Chalmers Wesley United Church. Others split into the Secession Church, the Relief Church and the United Presbyterians (as opposed to the Canada Presbyterians), who in 1875 merged with the Church of Scotland – and on it went. The Methodists included the New Connection, the Lady Huntingdons and the Wesleyans, and later joined forces with the Primitive Methodists and the Bible Christian Church. The Wesley Methodists built a gothic cut-stone church on St. Stanislas Street in 1849, now a public library. The Congregationalists had managed to find enough in common with the Presbyterians to join ranks with them in 1844.

While most of these new Protestant churches were staunchly anti-Roman, Bishop Andrew Hunter Dunn at the Anglican Cathedral was veering so strongly towards Rome that Rev. William Noble of the "low Anglican" Trinity Church wrote him a rude letter: "Your reckless aggression, as leader of the Romish propaganda in the Church of England, imposes on me a very unpleasant duty; but God, as well as England, expects every man to do his duty. The unparalleled audacity with which you are unProtestantizing the Church of England, and assimilating her into that of Rome ... demand a plain and fearless exposure." Another Anglican church with Romish leanings was the congregation of St. Matthew's on St. John Street (Rue Saint-Jean), which had replaced a converted gravediggers' house with an elegant medieval-style church, now another public library.

New Roman Catholic and Anglican churches and chapels were sprouting up like crocuses. The old bilingual chapel of St. Richard's Parish in Sillery, named after an English saint, was replaced by a new church in 1854, this time named after St. Columban, a favourite Irish saint among the Irish shipworkers in the parish (now named Saint-Michel). The same year the Anglicans of Sillery, who made up 10% of the town's population, built St. Michael's Chapel above the cliff, although some of the bourgeois families refused to go, populated as Upper Sillery was with riffraff such as gardeners

Methodist Church, Barbara O'Halloran, 1940.

Providing a fiery alternative to the literate and polite Anglican gentry, Methodism gave free expression to the religious enthusiasms of the marginal. Many celebrated American itinerant preachers came to Quebec, including the charismatic Lorenzo Dow with his six-inch-long red beard. He was known to preach for four hours and then snap his Bible shut and leap out of the window directly into the saddle of his waiting horse. At one time the city had three Methodist churches, including this one built in 1849. In 1941 it became the library and headquarters of the Institut Canadien.

and servants who worked in the merchants' villas. When the Redemptorist Fathers from Baltimore opened a Catholic chapel in 1885 down on Champlain Street, the Anglicans, not to be out-done, opened a Protestant mission there three years later.

St. Patrick's moved to Grande Allée in 1915 to serve the increasing Irish population in the Montcalm district, although the diehards at the McMahon Street church held on until 1967, when the parish could no longer afford to maintain two churches. The old St. Patrick's was burned down in 1969 by an arsonist, and served as a public parking lot until the Hôtel-Dieu Hospital built a research centre within the old walls of the church.

St. Matthew's Church.

St. Matthew's Anglican church (now the public library on Rue Saint-Jean) was one of the most important Anglo-Catholic parishes in Canada. Even its neo-medieval architecture harked back to the old Catholic Church.
It supported episcopal control in church governance, while evangelicals such as Jeffery Hale wanted more lay control. Canvassing for lay delegates for the new Anglican Synod (church government elections) was so contentious that there was a riot in the church in 1859. A mob armed with steel knuckles, slingshots and bludgeons rushed Rev. Henry Roe and dragged him from his seat. The police were called in to restore order.

St. Matthews Church Quebec.

Rival empires come to blows

The Gavazzi riots

The francophone Catholic Church in this era regarded the Enlightenment as an unfortunate historical blip that had unleashed atheism and anarchy, and saw the creation of a vast spiritual empire under the pope as the only hope for humanity. Thus, 30 years before Wilfrid Laurier was considering sending Canadian troops to fight Queen Victoria's imperial war against the Boers in South Africa, hundreds of Quebecers were busy signing up with the Zouaves to go and defend the extensive Papal States from being incorporated into the new country of Italy. Clergy in Quebec increasingly entered secular domains, gaining power over most francophone institutions. French was considered a sacred tongue because it was closer to Latin, and Protestantism was considered indistinguishable from freemasonry and Judaism.

From the beginning, Protestants looked at this Catholic trend with deep mistrust, and in 1853 anglophones of the two faiths came to blows. Tensions were already high as debate was heated in the Legislative Assembly over the clergy reserves, and George Brown, the influential editor of the Toronto *Globe*, had just proposed abolishing Catholic schools. In June 1853, Italian renegade priest Alessandro Gavazzi came to talk in Quebec City following a very successful speaking tour in Toronto. After a taste of his anti-Catholic polemic at the Methodist Church, other Quebec Protestant churches refused to host him. His principal advocate Jeffery Hale, however, persuaded the brand new Chalmers Free Church on St. Ursula Street to take up the challenge.

Admission was 30 cents, but this failed to deter 1000 people from thronging the church, and another 400 gathered outside. Protestants noted with alarm that there were many Irish Catholics present. When Gavazzi spoke of evil murderous priests and warned of a new Catholic Inquisition in Quebec, stones began to fly and a riot broke out. Women fainted, children began throwing Bibles and prayer books, and the rioters shouted "Pull him out! Have his heart's blood!" Gavazzi defended himself with a chair before he was thrown from the pulpit, head first. He hid in the basement while his assistant was savagely beaten. Although the police had been warned, their intervention was minimal, possibly because a large number of them were Irish. Chief Inspector John Maguire went off to call the troops, but fell into a deep ditch on the way. Dr. James Douglas and Mayor Ulric Tessier spirited the battered Italians back to their hotel. As Gavazzi hurriedly boarded his steamer the next morning, he narrowly missed being brained by a chisel flung in his direction.

Toronto editorialists wondered why, after such a show, the government should pay for Catholic health and education. Quebec Protestants wondered how to ensure that they could worship in their own churches without molestation, and several Orange Lodges sprang up in the city. The inter-religious tolerance of early-nineteenth-century Quebec City was deteriorating fast. The Quebec papers called it the outbreak of religious war.

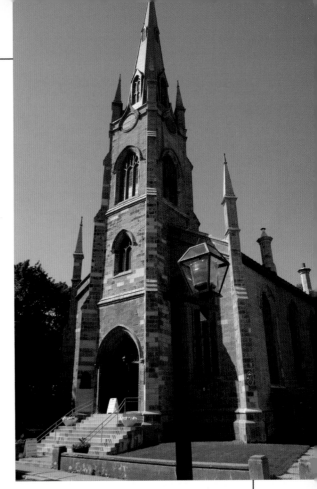

Chalmers Free Church (now Chalmers Welsey), Rue Sainte-Ursule.

Hugh Murray, Irish Quebecer and sub-lieutenant of the Zouaves, *L'Opinion publique*, 1874.

Alessandro Gavazzi, antipapal campaigner, 1809–89, J.H. Walker.

29

Benevolent ladies and Fenians

Charities and associations

After "Black '47", the year when so many Irish immigrants died in Quebec, the Irish community began to organize a host of charitable organizations and institutions, to which they soon added cultural, educational and political associations too.

In 1847, shipbuilder John Nesbitt and his wife had opened their home to children who were waiting for their parents to emerge from hospital, and later converted it into an orphanage. The parish priest Bernard McGauran opened St. Brigid's Asylum in 1856, and funds came from Catholics and Protestants alike. Originally it was intended for orphans, but it soon housed destitute men and women of all ages, as well as young people arriving from the country to look for work. The home was first run by Anna Bradley, daughter of a local doctor. When the Sœurs de la Charité took over management, the asylum committee complained the sisters were not buying their supplies from Irish merchants. This and other quarrels caused the Mother General, Mère Marcelle Mallet, to withdraw her sisters from St. Brigid's. When they were asked back again, in 1877, the committee stipulated that the sisters had to be English-speaking. Once they arrived, most turned out to be Irish anglophones, but there was nowhere for them to sleep.

While the residents of St. Brigid's were known to drink and quarrel now and then (Anna Bradley resigned in despair after someone hurled a knife at a servant), the Total Abstinence Society brooked no tipplers. The Hibernian Rifle Club taught its members to shoot, and the Hibernian Cadet Corps gathered young men to learn the Irish language, history and music. The women of the parish organized the St. Patrick's Ladies' Charitable Society to help their destitute compatriots, and the parish priest started a penny savings bank for those who had anything left over from their meagre wages at the end of the week. The St. Patrick's Literary Institute (1852) held musical soirées annually for over a hundred years, at which entertainment was provided by the church choir and the Emerald Independent Band, and later Joseph Vézina with the fledgling Orchestre Symphonique de Québec, founded in 1902.

Social life and politics were closely linked, and the St. Patrick's Literary Institute on St. Anne Street also brought together undercover Fenians, as did the Hibernian Benevolent Society. The Quebec City Fenian cell, whose goal was to use force to liberate Ireland from the British, tried to incite both Irish and French Quebecers to rise up against the crown. With very few members of the Irish Protestant Orange Order to blow the whistle on them, the Quebec City cell was one of the most powerful in Canada. Unlike in the United States, membership in Quebec, still a British colony, was high treason and punishable by death.

The Protestant women of the city were no less active. The Irish founded the Irish Protestant Benevolent Society in 1859, and the same year the Ladies' Protestant Benevolent Society built the Ladies' Protestant Home, a fine neo-Italian Renaissance building on Grande Allée, in which many Scots, Irish and English domestic servants ended their days. The home ended its own days in 1989, when the new St. Brigid's Home became the old people's home for all anglophones, whatever their religion.

Charity didn't just consist in building institutions. Anglophone women in Quebec City formed 49 associations in this period, 20 in the 1890s alone. Some offered "outdoor relief," or practical help to the poor in their own homes. The Quebec Mothers' Association was formed in 1847 to help poor women in educating their children, sewing, cooking and generally learning how to manage a household. In 1881 it became the Quebec Ladies' City Mission, which was still in operation when the Citadel Foundation brought together the remaining assets of many anglophone institutions (including the High School of Quebec, the Lake Edward Sanatorium, the Female Orphan Asylum, the St. George's Society, the Irish Protestant Benevolent Society and the Quebec Playgrounds Assocation) into one in 1976. The Women's Christian Association (later the YWCA) opened a refuge for "fallen women" (the Magdalen Asylum) and an Industrial Home where single female immigrants could stay in safety and get help finding a job in domestic service or the new factories.

Advertisement for the 39th Annual Soirée, *Morning Chronicle*, March 14, 1895.

The St. Patrick's soirées, beginning in 1857, attracted an ever wider audience. Local artists performed songs, poetry, concerts and plays. They were influenced by international artists who began their North American tours in Quebec City, but the content, the pathos and the patriotism were wholly Irish. In 1876, rival Irish literary societies put on three full-scale soirées. That year the Literary Institute moved into Tara Hall on St. Anne Street, formerly the site of the first Methodist chapel. This required some legal finesse as Jeffery Hale, a former owner, had stipulated that it never pass into Catholic hands.

Ladies' Protestant Home, Miriam P. Blair, 2003.

The Ladies' Protestant Home (1859) was a multidenominational institution owned, funded and managed exclusively by women for the benefit of "the indigent poor of Quebec City," especially immigrant girls and "respectable servant women who are destitute of funds." It also took in women deserted by their husbands and abandoned children, but refused shelter to "immoral characters, or intemperate persons of hopelessly confirmed habits." It had a large property which supported a herd of cows, an orchard, a flower garden and a potato patch large enough to supply the residents with 30 bags per year.

Finlay Asylum, Sainte-Foy Road, J.W. Love, ca. 1865.

The Finlay Asylum was built in 1862 by women from prominent Quebec City Anglican families such as the Sewells, Dunns, Mountains, Lemesuriers and Smiths, and sheltered destitute immigrants of all ages. Later, the children of anglophones working in remote areas lived there while attending English schools in the city. Former resident Pavel de Liamchin recalled that the dining hall was like a scene out of Harry Potter. The Finlay Home closed its doors in 1970.

Although its name suggests a certain exclusiveness, no one seemed to consider it odd that the last person to die in the Ladies' Protestant Home was a Jewish man, Edward Joseph. In his time he had been Justice of the Peace, Councillor on the Board of Trade and president of the Quebec Snowshoe Club, as well as president of Joseph and Company Ltd., the oldest wholesale grocery business in Canada. The Joseph women had for years worked alongside the Protestant women of Quebec City in the Red Cross Society and the Imperial Order Daughters of the Empire, and their children had all attended Protestant schools.

Many of the Jewish women also worked within the city's Jewish institutions. While the Beth Israel Jewish cemetery in Sainte-Foy dates from the 1850s, synagogues in Quebec City had an itinerant existence, the first one opening in the Masonic temple on Rue Desjardins in 1852, and from then occupying at least ten locations. With increased immigration early in the century there were two synagogues, one on Rue des Fossés (now Boulevard Charest) and another on Rue Saint-Dominic, and women formed their own organizations, such as Hebrew Ladies' Aid and synagogue sisterhoods, to help the new immigrants.

Orphans in London on their way to Canada, *L'Album universel*, 1906.

From 1869 to 1939, around 100,000 children were removed from single-parent families, orphanages, workhouses and the streets of Britain and sent to Canada. With the slogan "The Bible and spade for the boy; the Bible, broom and needle for the girl," the idea was that poor children would have better futures in the colonies – indeed that unless they were removed, Britain's "seething mass of human misery" might breed revolution. Once they arrived in Quebec, those considered undesirable ("some from disability but most on moral grounds") were sent back. If accepted, girls were put to work as domestic servants or "mothers' helps."

St. Brigid's Asylum, Grande Allée, Valentine & Sons Publishing Co.

In 1846, Father James Nelligan rented a house on St. Helen's Street (now McMahon) in which to shelter the many destitute Irish children arriving in town, and put up extra wooden sheds in the churchyard. St. Brigid's Asylum opened in a rented house on St. Stanislas Street in 1856, and then moved into an old barracks on Grande Allée. A chapel was added in 1870, a steam-heated laundry and stables in 1882, and classrooms so the 60 resident children could go to school. The institution was by then a vibrant and autonomous community that rivalled the old Irish neighbourhood on McMahon Street.

Three cardinal rules

The Jeffery Hale Hospital

While the Anglicans of some congregations wanted to keep their institutions strictly Anglican, Jeffery Hale was an evangelical from Trinity Church who collaborated enthusiastically with Protestants of other denominations in many philanthropic projects.

Until 1867 there were no hospitals for anglophones who weren't sailors, soldiers or immigrants. When Hale died he left a bequest for the establishment of a hospital to "treat the sick and disabled of the Protestant religion, without distinction among the denominations," that would "remain in perpetuity under the control of Protestants." At first it consisted of a converted house on St. Olivier Street (now Rue des Sœurs-de-la-Charité). The rules were that no one was to be admitted if they were contagious, incurable, or Catholic.

A year after the hospital was founded in 1867, the money had run out. The Board of Governors, including Baptist minister David Marsh, preferred that the hospital shut down rather than stoop to asking for government money. Within five years they were taking in paying patients, creating a two-tiered health care system.

The Protestant elite of the city also stepped into the breach, including Mrs. Pierce and Miss MacPherson. When Miss MacPherson's cousin, James MacPherson Le Moine, visited the new hospital, he reported on the polished floors "in brightness and glistening purity," the hot and cold water in the taps, and an impressive steam furnace which "looks a complicated piece of machinery, and big enough to blow the little institution into atoms, were it to turn rusty." He noted private and public wards, two children's wards and separate "fever wards" for the contagious. David Marsh had broken the first rule already.

Nursing School, Jeffery Hale Hospital, ca. 1910.

Inspired by Florence Nightingale, Quebec City's first nursing school opened at the Jeffery Hale Hospital in 1901. In his address to the graduating class of 1907, G.M. Fairchild warned the nurses against three major faults: trying to usurp the place of the doctors, gossiping about what they saw or heard in private households and becoming drug addicts: "The drug habit is the one to be most feared." A contemporary training manual encouraged nurses to cultivate their minds by "hearing good music, visiting picture and art galleries and witnessing good plays," so they could converse intelligently with convalescing patients.

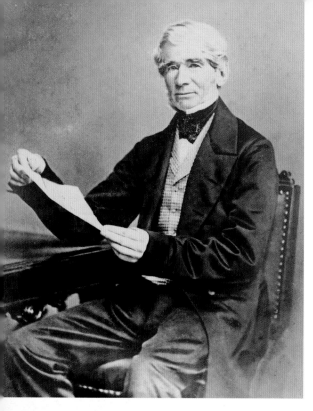

Women were the mainstay of the hospital. Elizabeth Bignell directed nursing care and finances from 1886 to 1901, and Ethel Hale, niece of the founder, gave money for a surgery department. Elizabeth McKenzie Turnbull, whose father James McKenzie operated the Lévis horseboat ferries, gave money for a maternity ward, a nurses' residence and long-term care facilities. The second of the three rules, incurability, was now broken too.

With donations from William Price, James Gibb Ross and James Douglas, Jr. (son of the founder of the Beauport Asylum), the hospital moved to a new building on Boulevard Saint-Cyrille in 1901. By 1906 it began taking in Catholic patients – the thin edge of the wedge. In 1911 the hospital hired nurse Emily Fitzpatrick. She was the sister of the Chief Justice of Canada, Sir Charles Fitzpatrick, and she was also a Catholic. The last rule had been broken.

Jeffery Hale (1803–1864), William Notman, ca. 1860.

Born in Quebec City, Jeffery Hale was educated in England and joined the British Navy at the age of 12. Deeply pious from his youth, he deplored the immoral life of the sailors, mistrusted British foreign policy and eventually left the Navy in disgust, asking, "What is warfare but legalized murder?" He blamed absentee landlords for the state of Ireland and was fiercely opposed to slavery. On his return to Quebec City he founded several schools, including the first Sunday school. Here poor working anglophones could receive an education, and in his Provident and Savings Bank they could save their money.

Jeffery Hale Memorial Hospital, Valentine & Sons Publishing Co.

In 1901 the Jeffery Hale Hospital moved from its cramped quarters on Rue Saint-Olivier to a vast new property enclosed by Boulevard Saint-Cyrille (now René-Levesque), Lockwell, Turnbull and Claire-Fontaine streets. In 1906, doctors began to specialize: surgeons, radiologists, anesthetists, urologists, gynecologists and pediatricians divided into their separate domains. When the hospital moved again in 1955, the old premises became a police station, a morgue and a courtroom. In 1980 it was converted into apartments.

Jeffrey Hale Memorial Hospital, Quebec

All that man's ingenuity has yet brought to light

Anglophone intellectuals at the Lit and Hist

A reporter for the *Morning Chronicle* in 1875 described the book-shelves of the Literary and Historical Society as containing "the essence of almost all that human intelligence, human thought, human wit, man's invention and ingenuity has yet brought to light."

Society members felt that within these walls they were at the apex of the civilized world. Every member was an amateur artist, scientist, historian, poet, botanist or educator. The list of lectures given at the society provides an indication of these people's amazing intellectual ambition and energy. They spoke on ancient Greek drama, copper deposits, birds' eggs, French-Canadian genealogy, trigonometry, Finnish sagas and ostrich farming in South Africa. One night in 1861 E.T. Fletcher, perhaps a precursor of modern linguist Noam Chomsky, lectured on "Languages as Evincing Special Modes of Thought," and in 1862 members attended the intriguingly entitled lecture "The Skin and its Appendages," given by Dr. John Racey. These topics weren't always received with the respect that they deserved. That year the *Quebec Gazette* reported that "the great mass of the fashionable audience ... seemed to ignore the presence of the lecturer, and chatted and laughed and paraded about the Hall in the most perfect oblivion of all that was going on upon the platform."

The society had in its possession many important historical documents, from both the era of New France and later. It thus attracted aspiring historians such as William Smith, William Kingsford, Francis Parkman, William Wood, James MacPherson Le Moine, George Gale, A.G. Doughty, G.M. Fairchild, Frank Carrel and Blodwen Davies, all eager to interpret Canadian history in their own way, and specifically to forge the English and French histories into a single, heroic past, with the British Empire a logical successor to Quebec's glorious French heritage. They tended to romanticize the *habitants* and admire New France, and most were determined that the two nations would succeed in honouring each other. Some of them were brilliant and accurate, others were interesting but wrong, and others were both boring and wrong.

Still, they loved their history. At the centenary celebration of Benedict Arnold's 1775 attack on Quebec City, fought off by French and English speakers together, society members held a ball at which they all dressed up in period costume. Mr. Dunn wore the belts of a man who was killed in action in 1775, still stained with his blood. Society members took great delight in their artefacts and preserved them with care, although they were repeatedly culled by fires. The natural history collection was sold to the High School of Quebec in 1890 for $200, other artefacts were sold to the provincial government in the early twentieth century, and several paintings and manuscripts were auctioned off at Christie's in the cash-strapped 1980s.

Interior of the Literary and Historical Society of Quebec.

Founded in 1824, the Society was dedicated to cultivating art and literature and preserving Canadian historical documents, objects and sites. The society was midwife to several national cultural institutions, such as the Historic Sites and Monuments Board of Canada, the Geological Survey and the Public Archives. In 1870, Henry Miles addressed the society on the need for a Canadian archives, and the following year at the society's request drafted a petition to Parliament signed by 60 of its "authors and literary inquirers." The first public archivist began work in Ottawa with three empty rooms, no assistants and no documents.

From the Misses Joseph :—A Loon's Egg found at Rivière du Loup *en bas* 1 ; English Farthing, 5 and 10 centimes, Belgium ; Ten and Two centimes, Italian ; Five, Two, and One centimes, France ; a Five centime French Republic ; Twenty, Ten, Five, Two, and One Centimes, Switzerland ; Two pieces Lava from Mount Vesuvius ; One piece of Brick taken from a House in Pompeii ; One piece of Lava from the excavations in Pompeii ; One twisted Shell from Mobile ; One Starfish from Rivière du Loup *en bas.*

" J. McLaren, Esq. :—Some petrified Shells from Mingan Islands, North Shore, St. Lawrence.

" Dr. Marsden :—A Squid or Ink Fish.

" Dr. Bligh, through Dr. Marsden :—The Fangs of a Rattlesnake.

" J. K. Boswell, Esq :—A Sheldrake ; a Black Woodpecker.

" C. Lindsay, Esq :—A Ten Centime of Charles X.

DONATIONS TO THE MUSEUM.
1874.

Captain Jephson, R.N. :—Silver Coin of Emperor Maximilian ; Two Moorish Bronze Coins of 1288.

W. Marsden, M.D. :—A very old Coin.

J. Gillespie, Esq. :—A piece of Iron Pyrites.

C. N. Montizambert, Esq. :—A Picture of the Old Recollet Church, Quebec.

J. Fraser, Esq. :—Two Teeth of the Megatodon.

W. Hunter, Esq. :—Seven Indian Arrow Heads.

A. Sandham, Esq. :—A Medal of Young Men's Christian Association, Montreal.

W. Marchand, Esq. :—Two Rebellion Half Dollars, 1837-8.

C. Tessier, Esq. :—A Coin of the Reign of Elizabeth ; a Coin of the French Republic, 1792 ; a Medal of Napoleon III.

Major Slone :—One Liard de France, 1657 ; One Silver Coin of ancient Date.

An Old Stadaconian :—A Box containing Specimens of Sea Weed, Coral, Sponge, Star Fish, &c.

L. McKay, Esq. :—A Brick from Nineveh, covered with Cuneiform Characters.

DONATIONS TO THE MUSEUM.
1875.

From P. Poulin, Esq :—Horns of Chamois ; Rosary from Jerusalem.

" G. Vogt, Esq. :—Silver coin of Chili ; Italian Coin of Napoleon ; I Russian Coin.

" Mrs. Algernon Sewell :—Knife from India.

From J. S. Budden, Esq. :—Grape Shot Found on the Plains of Abraham.

" J. C. Cattanach, Esq. :—Silver Coin of the Republic of Haiti.

" A. Graham, Esq. :—Medal of George I.

" H. Dinning, Esq. :—Model of the " Royal William," first steamship that crossed the Atlantic—built at Quebec.

" R. Craig,—French Silver Coin found in the ruins of a house at St. Foye.

" Rev. C. W. Rawson :—Two copies reprints of the " Times."

" Col. J. F. Turnbull :—Reprints of the first copy of the " Times " and other newspapers.

" Prof. J. Douglas :—Tablet with Cuneiform Characters.

DONATIONS TO THE MUSEUM.
1876.

From Rev. H. D. Powis :—Two Specimens of Herpetology.

" Prof. A. N. Macquarrie :—Copper Coin of 1781.

" H. N. Jones, Esq. :—Copy of the " Times," 1805.

" Prof. J. Douglas :—Massachusetts Spy, (newspaper), 1776.

" A. P. Wheeler, Esq. :—Specimen of Ichthyology.

" R. S. M. Bouchette, Esq. :—Twenty Specimens or *fac-similes* of Confederate paper currency in circulation in the early part of the late war, United States.

" W. A. Holwell, Esq. :—Fruit of the Monkey Tamarind ; Section of Lace-bark-tree ; Two pieces of Chewstick, Powder of Chewstick, (in bottle ;) Basket and Strainer made from the Wild Cucumber ; Circassian Beans ; Job's Tears ; also a Descriptive Catalogue of the exhibits sent from the Island of Jamaica, to the Centennial Exhibition, 1876.

DONATIONS TO THE MUSEUM.
1877.

From Jas. Stevenson, Esq., President :—The receipt of the Quarter-Master of the American Army, encamped before Quebec, in Dec., 1775, for two tierces of rum and two barrels of fish, certified by Brigadier-Genl. Arnold.

From E. Fales, Esq. :—Tooth of a Walrus.

From J. J. Foote, Esq. :—The autographs of Lord Brougham and the Right Honble. Geo. Canning.

From W. Moody, Esq. :—Two paper " quinze sous " of 1837, dated at St. Luc.

From H. S. Scott, Esq. :—A piece of marble from the coffin of Robert the Bruce ; two commissions bearing the autographs of George III, and of Sir R. Abercrombie, respectively ; also, a coin of Pius IX (silver,) two new German coins, and two specimens of Italian paper money.

**Literary and Historical Society:
Donations to the Museum, 1874–77.**

A modern fetish for categorization seems conspicuously absent in the eclectic collections of the Literary and Historical Society, whose members brought along whatever struck them as interesting, from bricks to teeth to works of art. It was up to the curator to "class and arrange them in scientific or methodical order," but they were exhibited promiscuously in a single room. Lectures given that year also demonstrated an enthusiasm for knowledge of every kind: Commander Jepherson spoke about "The Inner Life on board a man-of-war" and E.T. Fletcher on Savonarola, the 15th-century Dominican friar famous for the Bonfire of the Vanities.

Not playing together

Anglophone education

An education act specifically designed for Quebec in 1846 was the first legal recognition that Catholics and Protestants needed separate school systems, a recognition that was enshrined in the British North America Act of 1867. Unlike in the other provinces, Quebec's two major religious groups managed to steer their education systems clear of state interference until the 1960s, Catholics because they feared that mixing politics and education might lead to secularization, Protestants because they feared that a French-Canadian majority in the legislature might extinguish their English education rights.

But there was an increasing population that fit neither into the French Catholic nor the English Protestant camps, namely, Irish Catholics and Jews. Pluralism was seen as a threat to traditional Catholic values, and Catholics were only too happy for Jews to become "honorary Protestants" for the purposes of education. In the

Protestant schools Jews could have Hebrew classes paid for by the school board, but could not teach or sit on the board. English-speaking Catholics eventually won the right to English Catholic schools, but they were administered by French Catholic school boards.

By 1869 Catholics and Protestants each had their own separate school boards, so fewer and fewer Catholic and Protestant children knew each other, spoke to each other or played with each other. Their educational systems were quite distinct too. Catholics concentrated on French private classical colleges for boys, run by religious communities and leading to university, while Protestants ran English public secondary schools that put more emphasis on technology, commerce and the applied sciences. Their students were likely to land the better jobs in a city where, in 1901, more than 14% of the city's population could neither read nor write.

Irish boys now had their own anglophone Catholic schools, but until the founding of the Leonard School in 1935, Irish girls went to convent schools run largely by French-speaking religious communities, where a few classes were taught in English by Irish sisters or laywomen. In 1871, for example, 87 Irish girls were studying with the Ursulines, and 266 with the Grey Nuns (Sœurs de la Charité). On St. Patrick's Day the Irish girls were singled out for special treatment, sometimes getting the day off, or performing a concert of Irish music for the whole school and having a special treat at supper.

Anglophone girls in the Protestant system were able to attend free public high schools up to grade 11 and then go on to university. By 1917 there were more women than men in McGill's arts faculty.

With women's education came the hope that the end of their financial vulnerability was in sight. In 1893 a Miss Binmore wrote to the *Quebec Educational Record* that "it is no longer absolutely necessary that every woman in the family should be dependent on the men – to be reduced to unknown straits and intolerable suffering on the death of the latter." However, their prospects of getting a decently paying job were still slim. Women teachers were paid half of what men were.

Unlike in Britain, where children were to be "seen and not heard," schoolchildren in Quebec conversed freely with their teachers, observed a Scottish educational consultant to the Protestant School Board in 1901. While Canadian history was poorly taught, he said, British, Greek and Roman history were well taught "chiefly because the teachers know more about them." Textbooks on Canadian history were so bad that he recommended teachers teach it orally instead. "Canadian history at the early stages – at what may be termed the Heroic Period – is interesting enough," he wrote. "But it soon becomes a record of constitutional changes which are in themselves intensely dull for young people."

Crowd outside St. Patrick's Church, with St. Patrick's School on left. McMahon Street, ca. 1895.

Irish boys could go to the free school for poor children run by the Christian Brothers on Rue des Glacis (1843) or the Diamond Harbour or Foulons School on Champlain Street (1851), where classes were in French and English. In 1884, the two merged on McMahon Street at St. Patrick's School, built by the Redemptorist Fathers. Persecution of Catholics revived in the United States in the 1850s with the Know-Nothing movement, bringing in its wake church burnings, attacks and an attempt to burn down the Ursuline Convent in Galveston, Texas. Many American Catholics moved their children to Quebec.

Commercial Academy, *Album Le Voilier*, 1934.

In 1862, the priests at St. Patrick's parish and Notre-Dame-de-Québec invited the Christian Brothers to set up a fee-paying Catholic anglophone high school. They were worried at the number of Catholic anglophones attending the High School of Quebec and risking Protestant contamination. Some Protestant clergy suspected the Christian Brothers, who were all American, of "exciting revolt against the sovereign authorities," but in spite of a request to the Legislative Assembly that the revolutionary Brothers be sent home, they opened the highly successful Quebec Commercial Academy in the National School building on Rue d'Auteuil the following year.

Mental training of a high order

Joseph Morrin and his college

For a short time, some English speakers could attend university in Quebec City in their own language, through an affiliate college of McGill University.

Dr. Joseph Morrin was a Scots doctor who was already famous around town for being part of the group that founded the first medical school in the city in 1848 in the vacant City Hall on St. Louis Street. The medical school gave 120 public lectures a year in both French and English, and Morrin went on to help convert it into the Laval medical faculty in 1852. In 1855 he was elected mayor of Quebec City, and under his leadership the population was edified by new street lighting, a reorganized police force and the building of more than 11,256 plank feet of sidewalks, which meant that at last, at least in some parts of town, you could walk around without being up to your knees in mud, rotting vegetables and horse manure.

He also argued forcefully, to the extent of carrying a letter to London, that Quebec City should remain Canada's capital. Quebec City could more easily defend itself from those horrid Americans with their dangerous republican ideas than could other Canadian cities which, he wrote, were too close, and might "imbibe political opinions adverse to the integrity of the Empire."

He was the Hôtel-Dieu Hospital doctor, and a devout Presbyterian in the theologically moderate tradition, his best friend being a francophone Catholic priest. The Hôtel-Dieu sisters wanted to convert him to Catholicism, and would have managed, says historian P.-G. Roy, had his second wife not been so fiercely sectarian that she refused to let his friend the priest into the house.

Just before he died Morrin sold his share of the Beauport Asylum, Quebec City's first attempt at institutional psychiatry, and gave the $80,000 proceeds towards the formation of a men's Presbyterian college. His wife, continues Roy, may have influenced him in this choice too, as he had recently been sick and "lost his intelligence." There were many claims on his benevolence: until the last minute, according to some, he had intended to leave his money to the High School of Quebec. Other friends said he saw a dire need for a maternity hospice in Quebec City, and starting a rival university to Laval seemed out of character indeed.

But Rev. John Cook, minister of St. Andrew's for nearly 50 years, was all for it. The first premises of the new college were the new Masonic Hall, until the old jail came free in 1866. It was renovated and adapted, and Morrin College, along with the Literary and Historical Society of Quebec, moved in. It had a theology faculty, an arts faculty and a law department, and in his inaugural discourse Rev. Cook declared it would offer a "general education which involves no peculiarity of creed or confession." The teachers were to be "Christian men" but most were Presbyterian ministers. The college turned out scores more, many of whom were sons of Presbyterian ministers. They lived upstairs in the building while they studied, and then were sent out as missionaries to sow the seeds of the Gospel in Quebec's hinterland. The college's poverty was exacerbated by an improvident generosity towards these rural Presbyterian boys: it gave them free rent, countless scholarships, and a remittance of fees whenever a worthy student was in need.

Many of the outlying areas had already been evangelized, however, by the large number of Methodist itinerant preachers who got to the Scots settlers before the Presbyterians did: many rural Scots, preferring the hellfire-and-brimstone sermons of the Non-conformists to the reasoned moderation of the Quebec City Presbyterians, became Methodists or Plymouth Brethren. What's more, Rev. Cook insisted that his divinity graduates pass the requirements of the Scottish Presbytery, while the Methodists trained their preachers faster and got them out into the field. As for the Anglicans, they had been poaching on Presbyterian territory for years: of the 30 Anglican clergy in Canada in 1827, 11 were Scottish ex-Presbyterians.

Morrin College never turned out a single law graduate, and most of its students weren't after degrees but were "partials" who preferred to attend an interesting evening class or two. In 1886 Rev. George Weir suggested the college begin to offer "mental training of a high order to Protestant females." Women were thus to join the arts classes, and it was hoped as a bonus that they would "act as a stimulus to exertion and perseverance on the part of the students of the other sex." Women and men studied in coed classes, unlike in other universities, and the first women graduated from Morrin College in 1889, 40 years before the first women graduated from Laval University.

In spite of the addition of women, the college was foundering, and the following year an even less successful enterprise was added to the pot, the Morrin College School. This would train boys expressly to be evangelical ministers, and would act as a feeder to the college. It lasted two years. Finally in 1899 the college agreed to accept non-Presbyterians on its board, but by then it was too late. The college governors that year reported peevishly to the national Presbyterian Assembly that it was surely entitled to more support, seeing as it was "an Institution fighting for its existence in the very citadel of a community especially antagonistic to Presbyterianism in all its aspects."

Morrin College had a brief burst of activity towards the end of the century, when there were more than 100 enrolments. Although in its day the college attracted teachers from Oxford, Cambridge and Edinburgh, in 1900 McGill withdrew its affiliate status, as it considered the theology professors inferior. The college expired with a genteel artistic flourish. Canon Frederick George Scott, the rector of St. Matthew's, taught a last English class, Miss Euphemia McLeod wrapped up her technical drawing course and Mr. Bishop gave the last biweekly class in harmony.

Dr. James Douglas, Jr., gave the college one last shot in the arm with a $5,000 grant, and it again had 102 students but, it was reported, they were "mostly women or partials," and after this final five-year sputter it went out.

Dr. Joseph Morrin, Théophile Hamel, 1864.

Joseph Morrin arrived in Quebec with his Scottish parents at the age of four. He was apprenticed to a Quebec doctor, James Cockburn. After further study in London and Edinburgh, he failed his exams for the Royal College of Surgeons, but obtained a licence to practise in Quebec. While perhaps no great academic, Morrin was a friend to the mad, the poor and the lost. He was the prison doctor and a founding member of the Beauport Asylum, and opened a sailors' hospital and later the Marine and Immigrant Hospital. A devout Presbyterian, he left money for the founding of Morrin College, where Quebec's anglophones could get degrees.

Chapter 3

Imagining Empire

*T*his was the era of Confederation, which gave Quebecers a country they could belong to that wasn't Britain. The identity struggle intensified with the British Empire trying to hold anglophone and francophone Quebecers together in its bicultural vise – or embrace, depending on where you stood. Tourists flocked to Quebec City, and hotels sprouted, including the Château Frontenac. Other buildings were destroyed to make way for new developments. Some people began to consider that a few of the old buildings, along with the Plains of Abraham, might be worth saving from developers; and new architectural styles reflected a nostalgia for the past. The tercentenary celebrations in 1908 brought together divergent groups for a brief moment of relative unity, soon to be disrupted by the conscription crisis of 1918.

When the seat of government of the new Dominion of Canada was bestowed on Ottawa in 1867, Quebecers keenly felt their city's loss of status, only minimally mitigated by its crowning as the capital of the new province of Quebec. Many Quebecers, such as Mayor Joseph Morrin, protested mightily. But as a consolation prize, anglophone Quebecers now had a country, and even an empire, to belong to.

These shifting sands gave rise to wildly divergent nationalisms. George-Étienne Cartier preached harmony between the two races at Confederation, in spite of their very different histories. "We would form a political nationality with which neither the national origin, nor the religion of any individual would interfere," he wrote. Jules-Paul Tardivel, however, felt differently. "What we want to see blossom here is French-Canadian nationalism," he wrote at the beginning of the new century. "Our people, for *us*, are the French-Canadians."

Levis from Quebec, Maurice Galbraith Cullen, 1906.

Maurice Cullen was born in Newfoundland, and spent his early years as a painter in France. Influenced by Monet and Gauguin, he brought Impressionism home to Canada, and particularly to the painting of Quebec winter scenes. He was accused of portraying Canada as a snowy wasteland, and criticized for painting snow in colours other than white. By the time he painted this canvas, however, Quebecers had begun to see their landscape as something other than a poor and bleak imitation of Europe, and to see themselves as a distinct and respectable people on the world stage.

"Dieu et mon Droit"

Governors general and the British monarchy

The new dual-ethnic state of which George-Étienne Cartier had dreamed was both French and English, but solidly part of the British Empire.

In a country that was composed of many nations, the British Empire was the "imagined community" with which many Quebecers identified. At its height the British Empire saw itself as the leading force for good in the world (as empires often do). "We happen to be the best people in the world, with the highest ideals of decency and justice and liberty and peace," the British diamond magnate and philanthropist Cecil Rhodes wrote in a letter to a friend in 1891, "and the more of the world we inhabit, the better it is for humanity." Distasteful as anything that smacks of empire may be to many modern Quebecers, being an imperialist for some was a new kind of freedom, and a preferable alternative to being British. Quebecer Anthony Price, writing of his grandfather Sir William Price, observed that "before the Great War, imperialism was an early expression of nationalism; Canada would be a full member of a community of peoples distributed throughout the world, united under the Union Jack, and no longer treated as a dependent colony."

A community of people needs a symbol of unity, and for Quebec that symbol was the monarchy. George-Étienne Cartier insisted the crown be placed at the very centre of the new nationality, and often claimed that French Canadians were of the Old, or Royal Régime, and even more monarchist than Upper Canadians. Royal visits abounded, and there was considerable francophone enthusiasm. After all, the British monarch's motto, *"Dieu et mon Droit,"* reflected the Norman ancestry of the British monarch herself.

Governors general made a point of speaking French, and most felt their posting would have been unutterably boring but for the French fact of Quebec. Lord Dufferin enjoyed Quebec City so much that he established the Citadel as the governor general's summer residence, which it is to this day, and built a summer house in Tadoussac. The governors general reintroduced several customs from the *ancien régime*, such as the New Year's levée and their privileged access to the cloistered Ursuline convent, where Lady Dufferin experienced a Protestant frisson of horror at being shown Montcalm's skull.

After viceroy of India, being governor general of Canada was the second most desirable proconsular position available in the whole of the British Empire. One governor general, Lord Lorne, was Queen Victoria's son-in-law, and another, the Duke of Connaught, was her favourite son. These peers transported all the trappings of monarchy with them, the table manners, the clothes, the social life and the titles and honours to which the Quebec elites, both French- and English-speaking, aspired. George-Étienne Cartier himself was made a baronet. In 1927 historian William Wood reviewed the success of the Canadian project with eugenic euphoria:

> *Quebec has been blessed. By nature her people derive from two of the greatest races of either past or present … the science and art of her social life have grown their Canadian flowers from a fine, historic, virile, Franco-British blend. May this good stock grow even greater: bred from the humanly fittest to reach the humanly best!*

Spencer Wood, near Quebec City, "B.J.," after Lemercier, ca. 1870.
Spencer Wood was built in 1780 and acquired by timber merchant and horticulturalist Henry Atkinson in 1835. In 1852 it became the residence of the governors general, starting with Lord Elgin. He added to his popularity by building a vast ballroom where he held balls, dinner parties and evening parties twice a week, occasions that nurtured fantasies of regal pedigree among francophones and anglophones alike. In 1870 Spencer Wood was ceded to the province to be the lieutenant governor's residence. The residence was destroyed in 1966 by fire, and all that remains of it today are its gardens, now called the Bois de Coulonge.

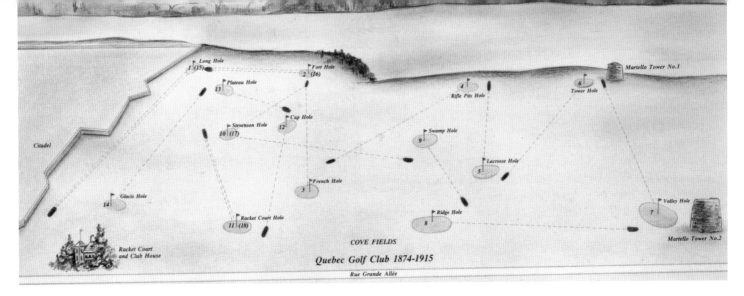

Quebec Golf Club 1874-1915

COVE FIELDS

Rue Grande Allée

Quebec Golf Club, 1874–1915.

A longstanding golf course on the Plains of Abraham – and indeed
the preservation of the Plains themselves – were among the legacies
of the governors general in Quebec City. The Earl of Minto interceded
to protect the Plains after Prime Minister Wilfrid Laurier signed an
order-in-council permitting the construction of roads and buildings on them,
and Earl Grey later urged the establishment of the Battlefields Commission.
When sprawling munitions factories began to invade the Plains, the Quebec
Golf Club (founded 1874) was forced to reduce the number of its holes.
Their names – "Racket Court Hole," "Lacrosse Hole" and "Rifle Pits Hole" –
testify to the conflicting vocations of the Plains. British golf champion
Horace G. Hutchinson nevertheless wrote in 1902 that the location of this
course was the "most entrancing" that he knew. "Indeed the golf is good,"
he added, "with dire penalties for the erratic and feeble." When the site
became a park in 1915, the golf links moved to the grounds of Kent House,
near the Montmorency Falls.

Putting Green, near Laboratory, Cove Fields, Quebec,
R.W. Rutherford, 1894.

Macaronic minds

Bicultural phenomena

Some anglophones at the close of the British colonial days did not even think of themselves as Canadians yet, let alone as Quebecers. William Wood complained of those who were "such persistant non-Quebecers in so many irritating ways. Even the Anglo-Saxon born [in Quebec] was an 'Old Countryman' ... he talked of the British Isles as 'home' even when he himself had never seen them."

This persistent Britishness was not universal, however. Anglophone Quebecers had by now been in sustained contact with French Canadians for a century and more. Moderately well-to-do anglophone families in Quebec City, such as the Jones family, had intermarried for generations at a stretch without giving up either culture. George Jones was a clerk who worked for the Jewish merchant Abraham Joseph. His father, a grocer in the Saint-Jean-Baptiste district, had married a French Canadian, Françoise Perreau, soon after he immigrated from England in 1815. In 1846, George married Honorine Tanswell. She was the great-granddaughter of James Tanswell, an English schoolteacher who immigrated in 1778, taught for 40 years in both French and English, and published a short-lived newspaper called *Le Héraut français*, the first in the colony to be published entirely in French. He, his son and grandson, all teachers, had all married French Canadians. These families moved with ease in both French- and English-speaking circles.

The children of these mixed marriages were truly bicultural. James MacPherson Le Moine was a tax collector, an ornithologist and a prodigious and entertaining writer of local history in both languages. He was perfectly at ease in both societies, with active memberships in both the Institut Canadien and the Literary and Historical Society. He was also deeply ecumenical in his person: he was baptized a Roman Catholic, was married in a Presbyterian church, was given a Catholic funeral service and was buried in Mount Hermon, Quebec City's Protestant graveyard.

Colonel William Wood, J.E. Livernois, ca. 1890.

There is a lively legend among Quebec City anglophones that William Wood, one of Quebec City's most prolific historians, was a direct descendant of Edward, Duke of Kent, and thus a contender for the British throne. The story goes as follows: the young prince Edward was in command of a regiment in Gibraltar, and on a trip to Geneva, met and married Marguerite de Saint-Laurent, Baronne de Fortisson. After they were transferred to Quebec City, she had a son, Robert, and when this was announced to George III, Edward's father, he ordered Edward back to England immediately, alone, whereupon the marriage was annulled. Their son Robert was given to a Quebec family, the Woods, to raise. Two memorial windows to Robert Wood were installed in Holy Trinity Anglican Cathedral, paid for, according to the legend, by the Crown. Edward married again, this time to Princess Victoria of Saxe-Cobourg, who gave him a daughter, Victoria.

***The Royal Engineers Leaving Pointe Lévis for the Red River, June 9,
1870, Léonce Cuvelier, 1941.***

When the Hudson's Bay Company sold Rupert's Land (the prairie provinces,
Nunavut and the Northwest Territories today) to the new Canadian
government in 1869, it neglected to inform the thousands of resident
French-speaking and Catholic Métis (descendants of unions between white
traders and First Nations). Their leader Louis Riel refused to allow
the appointed governor to enter the territory and established a provisional
government at what is now Winnipeg. The Royal Engineers in Quebec City,
along with 389 militiamen under Lieutenant-Colonel Louis Casault, set off
to put down the Red River Rebellion. No fighting occurred, and Riel was
able to negotiate the terms for Manitoba's entry into Confederation.

45

There was no uniformity of political persuasions, either among anglophones or among francophones. French-Canadian nationalists were less than enchanted with the empire business. Their leader, Henri Bourassa, believed that the new Canadian nation, an association of the "two mother-races of Confederation," was being hoodwinked into aiding and abetting a project of "world supremacy of the Anglo-Saxon race."

The Métis rebellion led by Louis Riel is generally regarded as an event that divided Canadians along ethnic lines, but the lines that were drawn among the residents of Sillery were more complex. Irish Quebecer Charles Fitzpatrick was lawyer for Riel's defence, while francophone Adolphe Caron, who was Minister of Militia in the federal government, sent troops to put down the rebellion, and did not resign when Riel was hanged for high treason in 1885. Colonel William Rhodes deplored the execution, while Mayor James Timmony supported Caron's position. Colonel James Ferdinand Turnbull and Colonel Guillaume Amyot each led a contingent of Quebecers to help put down the rebellion.

The respective cultures of English and French speakers were far from being hermetically sealed. Bilingual or *macaronic* popular songs containing both languages were heard in Quebec City's vaudeville theatres. English, Irish, Scottish and Welsh stories had also filtered into French-Canadian folklore, and after supper the traditional francophone fiddler included many an Irish or Scottish air in his repertoire. "Ti-Jean" Carignan, the famous *violoneux* from Lévis who inherited that tradition, learned many of his 7,000 tunes from his mentor, the Irish fiddler Michael Coleman, as well as from the Scot J. Scott Skinner. Modern Québécois pop and folk groups such as La Bottine Souriante, Le Rêve du Diable and Garolou show a strong Irish influence, and macaronic songs appear in the repertoire of Quebec City folk singer Tess Leblanc.

Even the currency was bicultural in Quebec. The new Canadian currency was issued in 1859, but until late in the century many storekeepers and workers still talked in pounds, shillings and pence.

Riel (Louis David Riel), Abbé Joseph Chabert, 1885.

Exiled after summary execution of a prisoner, Riel succumbed to mental illness and was admitted to the Beauport Asylum in Quebec City, where he stayed for two years. He had received "divine notification" of having been chosen as a prophet in 1874. "When I speak to you," he declared, "it is the voice of God that sounds ... I am the happy telephone who transmits the songs and messages of heaven." He went on to lead the Northwest Rebellion, and was executed for treason in 1885. His death caused ethnic tensions to flare, but loyalties in Quebec City were more complex.

Signs and statues

Language hegemony

The bicultural history of the nation was cast in bronze in the 1890s with the placing of statues of both Wolfe *and* Montcalm, Frontenac *and* Elgin in the niches on the front of Quebec's new houses of Parliament. But while there was representation at the national level for both French and English speakers, most francophones had to speak English to participate in public life. Although the population was less than 20% anglophone by the end of the nineteenth century, business and politics, town council meetings, public announcements and the signs around the city were still largely in English, including those relating to the new railways, trams and steam ferries.

In Sillery, the residence of Irish shipworkers, Scottish shipbuilders and many anglophone merchants, all the mayors between 1856 and 1913 were anglophone. Sillery municipal council continued to keep minutes in English until 1930. Nearly a third of Quebec City mayors, too, were anglophone in this period. Besides Scots-Quebecer Joseph Morrin, the first mayor to be elected by the people, there was the Loyalist-stock mayor who rejoiced in the name of George Okill Stuart (1850), later Judge of the Admiralty, and Thomas Pope, an "affable gentleman of the old school" and resoundingly Protestant in spite of his name. The tobacco merchant John Lemesurier, one of the Jersey anglophones whose Huguenot anscestors had settled in the Gaspé in the previous century, was mayor of Quebec City, as was Scots-Quebecer William Hossack and Irish-Quebecers Charles Alleyn and Owen Murphy. The Jewish merchant Abraham Joseph narrowly missed being elected mayor in 1858. The last anglophone mayor was Robert Chambers (1878–80), but anglophones continued to sit on city council. Brown, Lockwell, Dinan and McWilliam are all streets named after twentieth-century anglophone councillors.

In 1908, 450,000 people across the province signed a petition supporting a bill to make all public services, including the new telephone service, bilingual. The bill failed to make any headway in Ottawa, but two years later became law in Quebec. Language laws with any real teeth, however, were still a long way off.

A Victorian gallery: anglophone mayors of Quebec City, 1850–1880.

Horizontally from top left: George Okill Stuart (mayor 1846–50), Charles Alleyn (mayor 1854–55), Joseph Morrin (mayor 1855–56 and 1857–58), Thomas Pope (mayor 1861–63), John Lemesurier (mayor 1868–69), William Hossack (mayor 1869–70), Owen Murphy (mayor 1874–78), Robert Chambers (mayor 1878–80). By the 1890s anglophones were only about one twelfth of the city's population. In civic politics they had ceded much of their influence to francophone businessmen, but as a class continued to involve themselves in civic promotion.

"An older civilization than our own"

The Americans in Quebec City

While Irish, English and Scottish influence was still strong in Quebec City, new industries such as asbestos, aluminum, hydro-electricity and pulp and paper required capital investment that only Americans could provide. American capital and culture began to flow into Quebec, and Americans began to arrive as the bosses of the new industries that their capital was establishing.

Towards the end of the century the American presence began to shape Quebec City's architecture too. It was an American, Bruce Price, who built the Château Frontenac in 1893, Harry Edward Prindle who built Union Station (now Gare du Palais) in 1915, and Americans Walter Scott Painter and Thomas W. Lamb who built the Quebec Auditorium (now the Capitole Theatre). Americans also had an impact on landscape: it was an American engineer who had designed Mount Hermon Cemetery in 1848, and another, Frederick Todd, who designed Battlefields Park in 1908. Quebecers admired and hired American architects so frequently that Quebec City architects felt the need to set up an association (1890) to keep the work for themselves. Many Quebec City architects such as René-P. Lemay (who designed the École Technique, on Avenue Langelier) went off to the United States to study, and architect Georges-Émile Tanguay (Hôtel de Ville) combined an American with a French classical style in his buildings. St. Joseph Street was so modern, with its three new cinemas and its new department stores, that Quebecers called it the Broadway of Quebec.

Americans had also been coming to Quebec City as tourists in great numbers since the early nineteenth century, taking the standard continental tour via Niagara Falls and Montmorency Falls. With the railway now making Quebec City an easy and comfortable trip, they began to arrive in ever greater numbers, driven by curiosity, nostalgia for a bygone age and an entrepreneurial interest in the still undeveloped country. They and visitors from Europe carefully noted their observations and published them when they got home. American novelist Henry James, for one, saw Quebec City as "a hundred mementoes of an older civilisation than our own, different manners, ... social forces once mighty, and still glowing with a sort of autumnal warmth."

Bed and breakfasts and hotels small and large sprang up everywhere. Astonished at the pleasure tourists took in their dilapidated old town, residents began to look around them and say, hey, some of this old stuff is worth saving. Enterprising *literati* printed leaflets and tour guides, including the encyclopedic local historian James MacPherson Le Moine, who was only too glad to interpret the city for its visitors. The revived Quebec winter carnival of 1898 and the tercentenary celebrations of 1908 both took full advantage of the ancient customs and cultures of Quebec as tourist attractions, as Quebec City has continued to do.

Château Frontenac, Hazel de Lotbinière Boswell, 1938.

In 1892, the Canadian Pacific Railway, under William van Horne, built one of the most romantic and most photographed hotels in the world, the Château Frontenac, in the city's most historic and prestigious location, the old Château Saint-Louis. Architects William Lynn and Eugène-Étienne Taché competed to produce the winning design. But the prize went to Bruce Price, an American, who combined the picturesque silhouette of a French château with a very practical sense of the future: the five wings added subsequently did nothing to ruin its majesty or slow down the clicking of camera shutters. Quebec City artist Hazel de Lotbinière Boswell (1882-1979), granddaughter of Premier Henri-Gustave Joly de Lotbinière, based these illustrations for her 1938 book *French Canada: Pictures and Stories* on the style of traditional Quebec hooked rugs.

Calèche, Hazel de Lotbinière Boswell, 1938.

Americans began to arrive in Quebec in great numbers, and delighted in the exotic romanticism of the city. "Queer old Quebec!" wrote Henry Ward Beecher. "Here was a small bit of medieval Europe perched upon a rock and dried for keeping … We rode about as if we were in a picture book, turning over a new leaf at each street." The choice way to "ride about" has always been the calèche, which originally had only two wheels. In winter the hackmen or *cochers* wore picturesque buffalo robes belted with a *ceinture fléchée*.

Brochure for Hotel Victoria.

Turkish baths and Russian *bania* were fashionable in the United States, and a pleasant way to end a day of winter sports in Quebec. The owner of the Hotel Victoria, Benjamin Trudel, built a Turkish and Russian bath complex across the road from his hotel on Palace Hill in 1898. Not wanting his American tourists to have to go outside and cross the streetcar tracks to take a bath, he built a 12-metre overpass, but neglected to obtain a building permit from the city. He was soon forced to take it down.

Quebec sightseeing coach.

British tourists, steeped in the novels of Walter Scott, saw Quebec as still untainted by the industrial revolution, of which they were weary. British journalist Edward Salmon saw Quebec as "the most romantic spot in the British Empire." The one blight on the landscape was the English-speaking Quebecers, whom the British despised. "What with Irish nurses, and French and Scotch and American servants, the poor young Canadian can't preserve the English accent," wrote Lady Jephson in 1897. They had a "twang" that was "unequalled in all the world for its ugliness," and tended to have ideas above their social station.

Disgustingly studded boxes

Conservation and the new architecture

The politics of conservation have always been complex and controversial in Quebec City. Which aspects of history should be preserved, and which are dispensable? This question began to be asked in the late nineteenth century, and it is still being asked. The answer, of course, determines among other things *whose* history is remembered.

Some Quebecers wanted to knock down buildings to make way for landscape, while others wanted to knock down buildings to build new buildings. Some wanted to preserve old buildings; others wanted to knock down buildings to make way for pseudo-old things.

Governor General Lord Dufferin was less than enthusiastic about the new styles in American architecture. He was even more dismayed in 1874 when a delegation of the city's Special Committee on City Improvement went to Ottawa to present an urban redevelopment scheme that included the tearing down of the city walls. Lord Dufferin accused them of being "pettifogging shopkeepers" who wanted to flatten Quebec City "into the quadrangular monotony of an American town." By swinging his considerable weight around, Dufferin managed to save the walls:

> *By dint of using abusive language, calling them Goths and Vandals … I have succeeded in compelling [the members of the Special Committee] to agree to a compromise, namely, – to leave the walls … and to allow me to send them a very clever architect I know at home [William Lynn], who has a spécialité for picturesque medieval military construction, and who is to be allowed to finish off the breeches … with tourelles, towers, turrets etc, as may best preserve the ancient character of the enceinte."*

Thus the ancient character of the "enceinte," redolent of two royal regimes, was to be aided and abetted in its antiquity by some brand new, pseudo-old "improvements," as was the fashion in British architecture. The city's new "medieval" gates were in the manner of Queen Victoria's newly remodelled Balmoral Castle. One of them, indeed, was named after her father, the Duke of Kent. Old-timers may have remembered that he laid flat two Charlesbourg men with his fists when he was living with his regiment in Quebec City in 1791, but they also remembered that he was more comfortable speaking French than English. Tourists now regard these gates, British Empire remakes to the last turret and tourelle, as incontrovertible signs of the French *ancien régime* still guarding the old city.

Frederick Hamilton-Temple-Blackwood, 1st Marquess of Dufferin and Ava.

Quebec's domestic concerns were not uppermost in the mind of Lord Dufferin, Governor General from 1872 to 1878. He cared more about history, and had vast projects for preserving, beautifying and "oldifying" the city. He rebuilt the city gates, rebuilt the ramparts for improved promenading and expanded Dufferin Terrace. He planned to erect a new Château Saint-Louis on the site of the original headquarters of the governors of New France, in a similarly pseudo-gothic style as the new gates, but was unable to convince the federal government to pay for it. The Château Frontenac was built there instead.

Demolition of Porte Saint-Louis – 1871, Léonce Cuvelier, 1941.

The old gates that once kept out potential enemies were so narrow that
horses injured themselves and wagons were damaged. The first to be
demolished was the original St. John Gate. The military agreed to tear it
down on condition it be replaced, which they did in 1865. As soon as
the British troops left Quebec, the other gates began to fall. The St. Louis
and Prescott gates were demolished in 1871, followed by the Palace Gate
(Côte du Palais) and the Hope Gate (Rue Sainte-Famille) in 1873.

HIS EXCELLENCY LORD
DUFFERIN'S QUEBEC IMPROVEMENTS
KENT GATE

SCALE 8 FEET TO ONE INCH

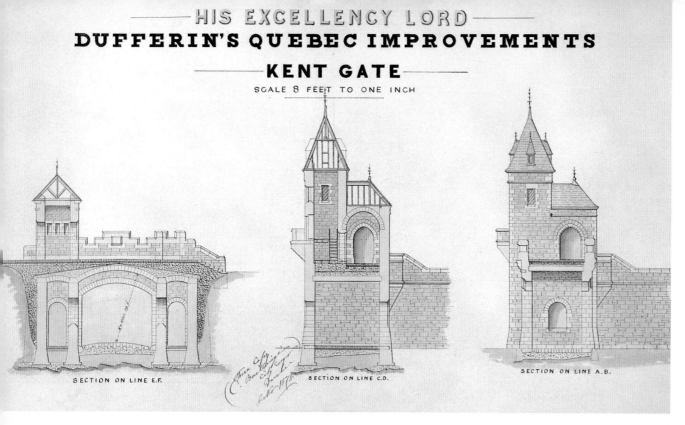

SECTION ON LINE E.F.

SECTION ON LINE C.D.

SECTION ON LINE A.B.

Kent Gate, Charles Baillairgé, 1878.

Proposed improvements to the fortifications at Quebec, William Henry Lynn, 1875.

Inspired by French architect Eugène Viollet-le-Duc, who had saved the walls of the ancient city of Carcassonne, Lord Dufferin fought city officials who wanted to demolish Quebec's gates and walls, and planned to make them a feature of Quebec instead. While Premier Boucher de Boucherville's government was busy tearing down the old Jesuit casernes to build a new parliament, Dufferin hired an Irishman, William H. Lynn, to build new "medieval" gates in the Franco-Scottish Baronial style. This was Old Quebec as Dufferin felt it should have been, with turrets and tourelles and fiddly details completely out of keeping with the severe 18th-century military blockiness of its original walls and gates.

Ross rifle factory, ca. 1905.

The various military installations on the Plains included Ross Rifles, a powder factory, a cartridge factory, a target practice range and a barracks. These may have struck the notables of the Literary and Historical Society as unsightly, but the fact was that Quebec City's arsenal employed 10% of the population. Ross Rifles remained in place until 1931, and the cartridge factory until 1939. The barracks were used as a internment camp for prisoners of war in 1940–41, and later as housing for homeless families. The last tenants left in 1951.

Cove Fields, J.B. Livernois.

The new interest in Old Quebec extended to the historical significance of the Plains of Abraham, and dovetailed conveniently with public health concerns. In 1907 the Commission of History and Archaeology, which included architect Eugène-Étienne Taché and historian William Wood, recommended the creation of an extensive national public park on the Plains. The man hired to design Battlefields Park was the American, Frederick Todd, who created a monarchist and imperialist version of the most republican of memorials, Gettysburg National Military Park.

Towards the end of the century the romantic conservationists at the Literary and Historical Society were contemplating how to beautify and historicize their city, especially in view of the approaching tercentenary. Champlain's *habitation* should be reconstructed, they said, and the Plains of Abraham were marred by sights that were distinctly unpicturesque. Everyone remembered the famous brothel, the Hotel Wolfe, at its entrance. Contemporary and menacing history in the form of Ross Rifles and other munitions factories, as well as a large prison full of criminals, were encroaching on a space upon which conservationists wanted to build a Quebec Battlefield Park.

But the Plains of Abraham could never fail to remind French Canadians of their humiliating defeat at the hands of the British. So in order to declare it a tie, the planners of the Plains established a second wing, Parc des Braves, to celebrate the Battle of Sainte-Foy, won by French forces in 1760. They named the whole *Battlefields*

Park. The two segments were originally to be joined by a long thin park which never materialized, although Avenue des Braves has managed nevertheless to retain a certain parklike nobility.

By the end of the century the city was a giant building site, and the new buildings blithely mixed several different historical eras together, as if anything old was better than the dull present. The Parliament buildings were designed to look like a Second Empire palace, the Armoury on Grande Allée to look like a French Renaissance castle, the post office on Buade Street to look like a French Classical *mairie*, and the banks on St. Peter Street to look like Greek temples. William Marsh hired Toronto architect Charles John Gibson to design a house on Grande Allée that was a baroque mishmash of styles all rolled into one.

Montcalm's house and the Old Skating Rink were unceremoniously knocked down to make way for modernity. Ironically, many historic houses were sacrificed to make way for historical plaques and statues. Some of the new buildings that were going up mightily offended the contemporary eye. William Wood described as "hideous, debasing and vile" the new "ungainly boxes" that were popping up everywhere, with "flat, stale, unprofitable sides, and sometimes disgustingly studded with meretricious gewgaws." He hoped that modern builders would recover from this phase, comparing it to the way "some educated whites revert from their own music to the lowest negroid jazz."

William Marsh House, 625, Grande Allée West, ca. 1900.

The house that shoe manufacturer William Marsh built for his large family on Grande Allée in 1899 (now the Vieille Maison du Spaghetti), with its massive verandas and vast semicircular rooms, was a baroque combination of many of the new architectural styles flourishing in Quebec. Dr. Canac-Marquis disapproved, advising that a single architect should supervise all new construction to prevent houses such as this "that refer to no single architectural style, are encrusted with towers or turrets like warts on a nose, and which combine monstrous mixtures of red and white brick."

British imperial hubris
The tercentenary celebrations

Earl Grey, yet another English peer, became Governor General in 1904. He pursued the binational vision further, and dreamed of fusing the historic virilities into one heroic race. Prime Minister Wilfrid Laurier, with his much deeper awareness of the complexity of Quebec society, looked on wearily as Earl Grey attempted to turn what was to be a local party marking the 300th anniversary of Quebec's founding into an international celebration of British empire.

Funding for Earl Grey's $2 million vision came from hither and yon. Even the schoolboys of England's most exclusive private (or "public") schools, Eton, Harrow and Winchester, reluctantly gave a shilling each out of their pocket money for the sake of Empire. Although he raised only a quarter of what he was hoping for, Earl Grey and his collaborators put on a show that was never to be forgotten in Quebec City. The tercentenary celebrations were the closest the two communities got to making a public truce. But the "historic virilities" stayed apart; full race fusion did not occur.

There were processions, fireworks, military tattoos, regattas, concerts, balls, church services, state dinners and garden parties. Most memorable were the massive pageants, arranged and directed by a pageant director from England named Frank Lascelles. England had its own divisions, primarily a rigid class hierarchy, and Lascelles's pageants were the latest fashion in breaking these down. Amateurs from every walk of life reenacted events from the glorious past in vast outdoor performances.

Performances were meant to be local, democratic and participatory, and thus Quebecers were both actors and audience. Arthur Doughty and Ernest Myrand wrote the script, which was entirely in French. Quebecers built the sets, designed the costumes (Charles Huot) and made them (Mrs. L. Williams, Mme Garneau and the Ladies' Auxiliary). William Price rounded up an army of 4,500 actors and extras. Joseph Vézina composed the music and the Quebec Symphony Society (ancestor of the Orchestre Symphonique de Québec) performed it. The Ladies' Auxiliary, working out of their headquarters in the Parliament buildings known as *Le Coin rose*, were in charge of logistics.

In his nationalist newspaper *La Vérité*, Jules-Paul Tardivel, a dedicated anglophobe in spite of his anglophone origins (born in Kentucky, he spoke no French until he was 17), depicted the tercentenary as a masonic imperialist plot to destroy the French-Canadian race. But even *La Vérité* admitted afterwards that the pageants had been "tasteful." *La Semaine Religieuse* went even further, claiming that French Canadians, perhaps for the first time, had been understood by outsiders: "Our English compatriots of all races, and the crowd of visiting tourists, especially from the United States, have seen with their own eyes the nobility and heroism of the founders of our French-Canadian race. All the English and Americans understood and applauded our glorious French and Catholic heritage!"

Iroquois who took part in the Quebec Tercentenary pageant, Keystone View Co., 1908.

Most popular of all at Quebec's tercentenary celebrations were the 100 First Nations families who were recruited for the pageants. Huron, Ojibwe and Iroquois dressed up obligingly in culturally inappropriate Plains Indian fringed jackets and feathered headdresses, and camped for the duration on the Plains of Abraham. Streams of curious visitors took delight in shivering with fear at the descendants of the murderers of Brébeuf and his brethren. Even though Aboriginals were most definitely not included in the aim of the "fusion of the races," they stole the show. The leader, American Horse, was a veteran of theatre, having taken part in the popular Wild West shows for several years. Unlike the Wild West show, this performance allowed the First Nations to win a battle in one scene, in which Dollard des Ormeaux failed to repulse the Iroquois at Long-Sault.

Dorothy Marsh in court dress, 1908.

Another prominently represented group was women, especially anglophone women, who took time from their busy schedules of visiting orphanages and organizing bazaars to dress up as French courtiers. They not only organized but also made more than 1,000 dresses and acted the roles, taking particular delight in playing French women of all classes from royalty to peasants. Forty-two per cent of civilian participants in the pageants were women. In contrast to the histories being written by their male contemporaries at the Literary and Historical Society, in this version of history women were highly visible.

55

Mustering power

Conscription and the Valcartier base

There was a large and impressive military component to the ter-centenary. More than 13,000 troops from three navies and the Canadian militias massed on the Plains. Naval ships from Britain, France and the United States dropped anchor in the river. The presence of eight huge British warships at the party was a clear message to Canadians to contribute to the British navy as if to their very own. The navy had just fought the Boer War, and the British wanted Canada to do its part, just as Harrow schoolboys had done their part out of their precious pocket money.

The strong hints anchored in the river did nothing to change the minds of the nationalists. The wines and spirits flowed generously between the elites on board ship, and the belles of Quebec City once again enjoyed the lively company of British officers just as they had a century earlier, but the strong feelings provoked by the naval debate signalled the end of the party. Wilfrid Laurier had graciously accepted the bribe of a knighthood from Queen Victoria in 1897, but he found the dancing was getting a little close, and feared that these overtures would lead to the destruction of the nation that he had worked so hard to build. Henri Bourassa was vindicated in his mistrust of the Empire. French Canadians were not going to go over to die so that Britain could dominate the world.

If the tercentenary was the high point of relations between the English- and French-speaking peoples in Quebec City in this period, the low point came very soon afterwards with the conscription crisis. At first neither francophones nor anglophones expected to be drawn into the war overseas that began in 1914. Quebec citizens of both languages had formed a Recruiting Association in 1916, but expected the Militia Act to be applied only to home defence. Recent immigrants were eager to join the fray overseas: more than two thirds of the volunteers in the Canadian Expeditionary Forces were born in Britain.

In 1913 the government had expropriated more than 5,000 hectares from 125 Irish farmers in Valcartier to serve as a provincial military training camp. William Price, having honed his mustering skills at the tercentenary, built a recruitment camp in 20 days for all Canadian troops being shipped to Europe, a feat for which he was later knighted. The women of the Imperial Order Daughters of the Empire tried to alleviate the confusion and apprehension among the more than 30,000 volunteers by working from dawn to dusk at Valcartier, running a canteen and providing entertainment.

"Our Canadian Troops" Canadian Infantry Men on Rifle Butts, Valcartier, ca. 1914.

In 1914 Valcartier became the mustering point for the more than 30,000 Canadian troops who set off to fight in World War I. In three weeks, under the direction of Quebec paper manufacturer William Price, the recruitment camp was kitted out with rifle ranges, sewers, a water supply, tent lines, latrines, roads and rail links to Quebec City. General Sam Hughes, meanwhile, gave contracts to his friends for 50,000 uniforms and 8,150 horses as well as thousands of Ross rifles, boots and harnesses. Target practice at the camp succeeded in blowing away the side of Pinkney's Mountain overlooking Lake St. Joseph.

The Military Review at the Quebec Tercentenary Celebration, Hider Kelly, 1908.

According to historian H.V. Nelles, this was "a celebration of an imaginary country, one which the organizers hoped to create." By inviting three navies to the party, Earl Grey hoped to teach Canadians pride in belonging to the British Empire – and also persuade them to contribute more to British naval defence. The Canadians, for their part, paraded 12,000 militia through the streets, hoping to convince the British that, having recently sent 7,000 soldiers to the Boer War, they had done enough. The Saint-Jean-Baptiste Society, whose idea the celebrations were in the first place, had withdrawn its support in disgust.

But when the time came to send the troops off to war, total disorder reigned under the command of the unpopular General Sam Hughes. Men were separated from their horses and stuffed on overloaded boats, and once they arrived in the killing fields of Belgium and France the Ontario-made boots and Quebec-made guns (Ross rifles) provided by General Hughes's cronies turned out to be woefully inadequate.

However much the military harangued young French-Canadian men standing in lineups outside the vaudeville shows on St. Joseph Street, they wouldn't join up. But Britain was at war and it needed men. Breaking all promises to the contrary, the government imposed conscription. French Canadians protested loudly, their protests culminating in a violent demonstration in 1918. Prime Minister Robert Borden, fearing that the Quebec City police might be sympathetic to the demonstrators, sent down troops from Toronto to quell the riots, troops who bludgeoned the "disloyal" demonstrators with their truncheons. "The whole of the lower town was in fog and darkness that night, and we heard shouts," wrote the poet Frank Scott. "Then all of a sudden we heard machine-gun fire, and it sounded as though there was a general massacre going on down there." Four people were killed and 70 injured.

William Wood saw this low in English-French relations, after the high of the tercentenary, as of a resolutely temporary nature, a "poison gas of ignorance, suspicion, anger and recrimination on both sides" let loose by World War I. But few French-Canadian families forgot the English-speaking agents who came to ferret out their young men from the woods or the barns where they were trying to hide. Meanwhile immigrant families from Germany, Bulgaria, Turkey, Croatia, Serbia and Ukraine were considered "enemy aliens," and were rounded up and kept at the Beauport armouries before being sent up to Spirit Lake, in Abitibi, to be held there at gunpoint until 1916.

Conscription, although singularly unsuccessful, shattered the fragile harmony between the races. In the 1917 election, for the first time, voters in the province voted overwhelmingly along an ethnic divide.

Recruitment poster, Gazette Printing Company, Montreal, 1914–1918.
"We will defend the precious jewel of freedom … Will we help crush tyranny? Apply to the Recruitment Office." This recruitment campaign did not hold much appeal for the approximately 85% of the city's people who were French-speaking, and may have had no particular affection for either England or France. When war broke out only 1,000 French-speaking recruits had signed up. Anglophones who signed up were mostly men born in Britain. "I remember one young man who got into train, his face was pressed against the glass and tears were coming down his cheeks," recalled Quebecer Marguerite MacDonald. "I always wondered whether that one came back."

Save us, boys!

The conscription riots

"There was an organized attack on the conscription office, in front of the Capitole Theatre. Three different groups marched up to the office – one up Abraham Hill, one down John Street and one up Palace Hill – and they met out in front. The police tried to prevent them from going in but were outnumbered. The rioters took a sign board and banged it over Detective Walsh's head. Then they went in and threw all the papers out of the second- and third-floor windows, and set the building on fire. Charlie Clint and I were standing on Kent Gate watching the proceedings. The firemen came down, but they didn't know how they'd be received. The crowd cut a couple of the hoses but then they let them go on. The firemen were always popular in Quebec.

"But then it got really bad. Soldiers were summoned from Ontario, and were stationed in the Citadel. When some trouble broke out, the battalion was called out. Charlie and I were at the corner of Esplanade and St. Louis Street when the soldiers came marching down in full battle order, and one lady became rather hysterical and fell on her knees on the street corner, shouting 'Save us, boys, save us!' But they just laughed at her. Then after that the commanding officer gave the command, 'Ten rounds load!' So it was getting kind of important.

"The rioters were guys of conscription age who hadn't yet been rounded up. It was pretty rough: the government had hired a lot of rowdies, tough guys, *des fiers-à-bras*, who went into the taverns down in Saint-Roch and rounded up guys who didn't have papers. The crowd got hold of one of these [government toughs], and there was a streetcar stopped at the corner of Crown and Joseph. They put him down in the track and wanted the motorman [streetcar driver] to run over him. They were pretty rough, the guys, you know. The motorman wouldn't. One of the fellows jumped into the streetcar and said 'I'll drive over him.' Someone else had enough sense to run around the back and pull the trolley down so the streetcar couldn't go.

"At the end of the riot they had a kind of an inquiry, and my father was head of the inquiry. They were mostly French people, and they drafted a paper saying that soldiers were responsible for the ones who were killed. They blamed the soldiers. Father said, 'You can't write a thing like that, that's going to make a lot of trouble in the rest of Canada!' They said, 'Mr. Scott, here's the paper, you write the report and we'll sign it.' Father wrote that unfortunately these fellows had been killed by stray bullets in exchange of fire.

"The last night of the riots, Father wouldn't let me go out; it was getting too rough. He said, 'You stay in the house tonight.'"

Guthrie Scott,
in an interview recorded
by Mary Ellen Reisner, 1985

My mother was terrified one of her sons would marry a French-Canadian Roman Catholic. There was a general feeling amongst anglophone Protestants that this would be a disaster … As for marrying a Jew, that was impossible … Marrying an Irish Catholic wasn't quite as bad.

Ronald Blair

In the past the Greeks wanted their children to marry Greeks, but I don't mind who my children marry, as long as they're happy.

Koula Aaron

People talk about the two solitudes, but the English and the Irish were two solitudes too. We hardly ever saw each other.

Patrick McKenna

1918 – 1976

Several solitudes

In 1871 anglophones had been nearly 40% of Quebec City's population; a hundred years later they were only 4%. While some had moved out of the region, many others had assimilated, with a speed unique to Quebec City. By 1971, about half the region's British-origin population spoke French as their mother tongue.

Life changed as much in Quebec City between 1918 and 1976 as it had perhaps changed over the previous century and a half. The Second World War, like the First, divided Quebecers into those who identified with the battle across the ocean, and those for whom it was a distant rumble. The economy changed out of all recognition, as did the composition of the immigrant population. Quebecers became "consumers," open markets gave way to the shopping centre, and housewives in the new suburbs experienced a new brand of solitude. Cars, movies, radio and TV changed all of Quebec City's cultures forever. Women were finally able to vote. Growing economic power and nationalism among French speakers resulted in British parliamentary customs, ingrained in Quebec public life since the Conquest, being banished.

Chapter 4

The Mall and the Fleur-de-Lis

The 1920s were a flurry of folly and prosperity for the favoured few. William Marsh's shoe factory was producing 9,600 pairs a week, the vaudeville theatres were hopping, and fashionable women, who hitherto had been expected to look pure, now started wearing long, narrow and shockingly revealing dresses.

Le premier péché, **Percyval Tudor-Hart, Leo Belmonte, Catherine (Rhodes) Tudor-Hart and René Baudonnet, 1926–1961.**

Montreal artist Percyval Tudor-Hart was a descendant of the English royal Tudor family and of Aaron Hart, one of Canada's first Jewish settlers. An associate of Toulouse-Lautrec and Matisse, Tudor-Hart opened art schools in both Paris and London. In 1935 he married Catherine Rhodes and came to live in Cataraqui, Sillery, which became a hive of cultural activity and housed a large collection of European paintings, furniture and Chinese porcelain. This tapestry, from a cartoon by Percyval Tudor-Hart, was the life work of Swedish weaver Leo Belmonte. They both died before it was finished, and Catherine (Rhodes) Tudor-Hart and René Baudonnet completed it in 1961.

Footwear and famine

The twenties and thirties

A shoe strike in 1926 sounded the death knell of Quebec City as Canada's shoe capital. The 3,000 shoe and boot workers, who were protesting against a 30% drop in wages, maintained their strike for nearly a year. The only anglophones involved were Roman Catholics, as international unions were being replaced by religious unions. Workers marched through the streets carrying banners depicting Pope Leo XIII, Cardinal Bégin, the Virgin Mary and St. Joseph. Management brought in American scabs to take their place. Many of the factories never reopened.

Cheap labour and booming hydroelectric power development attracted new businesses and allowed old Quebec City companies to expand. The white pines were gone, but Quebec still had a few smaller trees left that could be mashed up for pulp. The pulp and paper industry flourished, not least because in 1923 Quebec firms were paying the lowest wages in the North American newsprint world. Hundreds of hectares of marshland on the St. Charles Estuary were filled in to make way for the vast Anglo-Canadian pulp and paper mill. The firm's 580 employees swelled the old villages of Hedleyville, Smithville (Stadacona), Parkeville and New Waterford, all of which had been renamed Limoilou in 1893. Anglo-Canadian employees formed a successful hockey team, the Quebec Aces. When he wasn't playing forward for the less successful Quebec Duffers, William Price, grandson of the timber merchant, also turned his attention to pulp and paper. In spite of sound thrashings on the ice ("The Duffers dragged their weary selves off the ice, objects of the public scorn, covered with bleeding wounds ... Gore flowed like water," exaggerated a *Chronicle-Telegraph* reporter gleefully), his company did so well that in 1930 it built Quebec City's first skyscraper, 16 storeys high. Anglo-Canadian and Price Brothers were soon supplying newsprint throughout Europe and North America.

Many of the employees of the new industries were English-speaking, especially in the middle and upper management ranks. The insurance and banking sectors were also still largely controlled by the English-speaking elite. Many anglophones, old families and new recruits, now lived in "Montcalmville," a modern suburb replete with sewage and water facilities, where they could live, go to school, play and work entirely in English.

Côte du Palais with Victoria Theatre on right, Thadée Lebel, 1929.

Guthrie Scott remembered in 1985: "When I was very young, there were the silent movies at the Nickel Theatre at the corner of St. Anne and St. Ursule streets. The movies were very primitive: every time a roll finished you had stop the show to put on another reel, and they only charged five cents. Then as the thing was perfected they built the Olympia on John Street, the Victoria on Palace Hill and the Empire on Fabrique Street. By that time the show was ten cents."

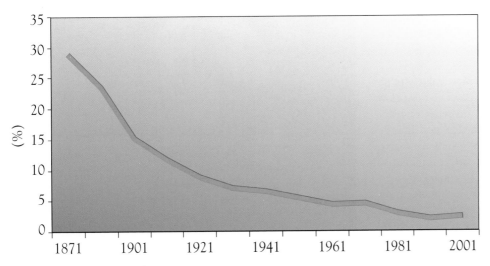

Source: Statistics Canada census information.

Note: A certain margin of error in this graph is to be expected as a result of changes in Statistics Canada data collection
methods and geographical boundaries over the years.

Decline of British-origin population of Quebec City as proportion of total, 1871–2001.

Counting Quebec anglophones has always been problematic. Until 1851 most population data came from religious events such as baptisms and burials. Non-Catholic denominations did not keep careful records, and the anglophone population was more mobile. Furthermore, until 1931, the census identified anglophones by asking about the origin of the first male ancestor who arrived in Canada. The United States, however, didn't count, and assimilation or bicultural origins were invisible. In 1931, a question about mother tongue appeared on the census, but this excluded people who spoke more than one language from birth, and people who had assimilated and moved into another language. In 1971, a third question solved some of the mystery: language most frequently used at home.

Advertisement in Quebec High School's magazine *The Key* for "Warner's Million Dollar Hold-Up" made by Parisian Corset Company, 1953.

Early in the century, long slim flapper fashions replaced boned undergarments, but in the 1930s the rounded "womanly" figure returned to fashion, and with it the corset. Dominion Corset, founded in 1886 by Georges-Élie Amyot, was producing up to 20,000 bras and corsets per day in the 1950s. Competition was stiff with several other factories in town, such as Ernest Ross's Parisian Corset Company on St. Vallier Street, his brother Gordon's Ross Corsets on St. Paul Street, and the Perfection Corset Company. Corset manufacturers even targeted high school students, as this ad in Quebec High School's magazine testifies.

By the 1930s the Depression had hit, and thousands of unemployed men were living in tents on the Plains of Abraham again, as immigrants had done as a hundred years previously. The city paid them 20 cents a day to build public amenities, such as a new water reservoir on the Plains and the Palais Montcalm with its swimming pool, library and 1,379-seat auditorium. The Salvation Army gave the Anglican minister's wife in Lévis 15 cents for every plate of bacon and eggs she served to the homeless and hungry men who got off the train from the Maritimes "in search of a square meal and a dry pair of socks." Quebec City's Irish community organized its own make-work project for the unemployed, who transformed an old barn behind St. Brigid's Home into a recreation centre. Parish members of St. Patrick's collected money by putting aside a cent for every meal they ate and donating it to the unemployed, while the Anglican congregation of St. Matthew's opened a soup kitchen.

Price House.

Built in 1930 in the heart of the old city, Price House was a symbol of the economic prowess of the new pulp and paper industry. In a city in the process of recovering its French roots, where French classical Beaux-Arts architecture was the fashion, the New York Art Deco style of the new skyscraper was an affront. "Quebec is not a big industrial city," complained *Le Terroir*. "Nor is it a Wall Street or a Broadway. It is a French metropolis, the capital of a province and a diocese." But city council voted for modernity, and the building went ahead.

Hobo's shack on banks of St. Charles River, W.B. Edwards, 1931.

Bertram Semple, a farmer in Little River (the farm is now a snow dump in Duberger), remembered in 1985: "During the Depression we saw many people with nothing. Our farm was near the poor section of the city. The people depended on snow shovelling in winter, and apart from that they made no money. They depended on the cabbages we couldn't sell for supplying their table. We delivered the cabbages to them in Saint-Sauveur: you couldn't expect a poor man to carry them home on his back. My dad had a kind heart. To this day I can go through Saint-Sauveur and be recognized for who I am."

Living Witness

Ronald Blair's ancestors came to Quebec in the early 1800s. Robert Blair, a Scottish agronomist who worked with Henri-Gustave Joly de Lotbinière on his agricultural innovations, was hired by William Price in 1842. Blairs worked for Price Brothers for the next four generations. Ronald has children (including the author of this book) and grandchildren in Quebec City.

"We lived near the top of Moncton Avenue, and our neighbourhood was all English-speaking. Down Moncton Avenue to Fraser just about every house was anglophone, including the whole of Learmonth and Lemesurier avenues. Everyone knew everyone. In Mrs. [Florence] Oliver's garden, there were paths, flowers, vegetables and raspberry bushes in the summer. In Stobo's Field we made forts and played football, and in winter we made an ice rink there. We played pretty much entirely in English.

"There were three or four French families, but we didn't know them. My mother was terrified one of her sons would marry a French-Canadian Roman Catholic. There was a general feeling amongst anglophone Protestants that this would be a disaster. One of my cousins by marriage wanted to marry a Roman Catholic. His father, the son of a Baptist minister, said he'd disown him. He married her anyway. As for marrying a Jew, that was impossible. I used to take Florence Pollack out to dances at the Habitant Inn on Sainte-Foy Road, but marrying her would have been out of the question for both families.

"Marrying an Irish Catholic wasn't quite as bad. Most of the Irish lived on Sillery Hill, or further down towards Parliament, but the McKennas, Irish Catholic, lived behind us, and the Timmons lived next to the Simons. In summer the Corpus Christi procession from the Dominican church would come by, and the Timmons erected an elaborate altar in front of their house. When the host went past everyone had to go down on their knees. If you didn't the rest of the crowd would force you to. We had Catholic maids at home, and they thought we were all bound for hell. Once they got to know us they felt badly about this, that such nice people should go to hell.

"When I was young, you could pretty well get along entirely in English even in Quebec City. Both my parents spoke French, but I knew people who were not originally Quebecers who could not speak a word of French, and they survived. I was taught French well at school, but I learned how to speak it with our maids, and on my first job with Price Brothers in the woods, where I was the only anglophone."

Ronald Blair

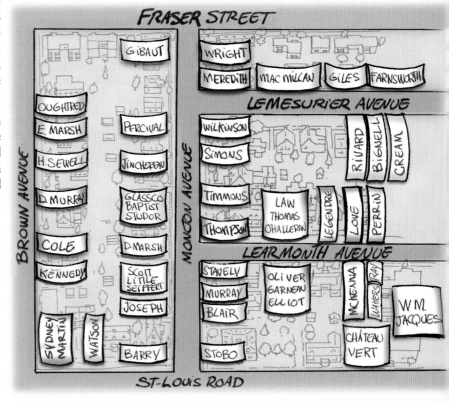

The anglophone Montcalm enclave, ca. 1935.

"An intermixture of foreign strains of blood"

Changing immigration patterns

In 1920 the Port of Quebec was still the point of entry for nearly half of all immigrants to Canada. Sixteen per cent were from eastern Europe, and there were Scandinavians, Greeks, Italians, Chinese and Portuguese, but most were still from Britain. The new heavy industries required boilermakers, machinists and blacksmiths, while clerical workers took jobs in the growing finance and insurance sectors. In the first three decades of the century, the number of British-origin workers in the province more than tripled.

As anti-Semitism rose in the 1930s, increasingly desperate Jews were prevented from immigrating. "We must keep this part of the Continent free from unrest, and from too great an intermixture of foreign strains of blood," said Mackenzie King. Canada had one of the worst records of Jewish refugee settlement in the world.

Immigration dropped in the Depression, and when it resumed after World War II, Quebec City was handling only a quarter of all immigrants. Many of them were now from parts of Europe other than Britain. When Chinese women were finally allowed to immigrate in 1947, the Chinese community moved from the laundry into the restaurant business. By the 1970s, St. Andrew's Presbyterian Church had long ceased to be the preserve of the Scots. The Clerk of Session was Dutch and the janitor was German. Among the congregation were a Jamaican high school teacher, a Hungarian architect and a Czech composer.

As the economy was still dominated by English speakers, and the Protestant schools had agreed to educate all non-Catholics, two thirds of the immigrants in the province sent their children to English schools. Although Jews were considered honorary Protestants, they maintained their own Hebrew schools too, such as Mark Gardner's Jewish School on Rue Sainte-Marguerite. Italians such as Luigi and Engelo Sgobba sent their children to English schools, as have succeeding generations of the families of early Italian immigrants to Quebec.

A generation later, English had become the first language of the new immigrants, adding new blood and new cultures to Quebec City's anglophone population. It was not only the new immigrants who were sending their chilaren to English schools, however. More and more French-speaking Quebecers were doing the same.

The Grikas

Anglo Greeks in Quebec

The first Greek immigrant to settle in the city itself was Thom Adamakis, who arrived in 1900 and sold fruit on Rue Saint-Jean. Louis Aaron arrived in Quebec in 1913 and in 1945, he and his wife Marina Pouloudi founded the Diana on Rue Saint-Jean, Quebec City's oldest Greek restaurant. There were 13 Greek restaurants in Quebec City at the time, including the famous Old Homestead in Place d'Armes, where Greek immigrant George Trakas wined and dined the Séminaire professors and other elites from 1929 on.

For three generations the Aaron family in Quebec City have married Greeks from Greece, spoken English as their second language and sent their children to English schools, although now all these traditions are shifting. "In the past the Greeks wanted their children to marry Greeks, but I don't mind who my children marry, as long as they're happy," says Koula Aaron, Louis's daughter-in-law.

Greeks from Greece were known as *hellenas*, as opposed to the Quebec Greeks, known as *grikas*, who were held slightly in suspicion by prospective mothers-in-law. Greeks lived downtown and spoke a particular dialect that blended Greek with English.

Louis Aaron and Marina Pouloudi.

Living Witness

Napoleon Woo is a hairdresser, a keen hunter, and the owner of the Wok 'n' Roll restaurant, one of the last Chinese businesses in what used to be Quebec's Chinatown. His father came to Quebec from Guangzhou in the 1920s, but his wife didn't follow until 30 years later, when Chinese women were first allowed to immigrate. His parents opened the restaurant in 1957. Napoleon describes his mother's religion as "Buddhist-Catholic." His daughter is a third generation of Quebec Woos who are trilingual: Cantonese, English and French.

"I was taken to St. Brigid's Home on de Salaberry when I was six years old. I had no English at all and my mother left me a bag of food. I didn't know if she'd ever come back. At least I've got the food, I thought, and I left it on the chair by my bed. We were 30 or 40 boys in the dormitory, and when I woke up, it was gone. That was a blow.

"We were treated pretty well. But there was an old guy called Joe who lived there, and he used to give out nickels to everyone, but when it came to me he'd say, 'There's nothing left!' Once I passed him in the corridor and said hello to him. He said, 'You dirty Jap!' and punched me in the stomach. I said to a nun, 'I'm not Japanese!' She said, 'Never mind about Joe.'

"The 'Home boys' used to have fights with the other boys at St. Patrick's High. We were the tough guys, from the Home. Lots were from broken families, or orphans, or their parents were alcoholics. I was lucky: another resident, Noreen Halton, was very kind to me, she became my surrogate mother.

"Although I went to St. Pat's I never went out with an anglophone girl, not even on a date. My girlfriends from school were all French-speaking. Perhaps it was because in school we were both minorities. One French girlfriend took me to her house at Christmas time. Her father decided to end the celebrations early, and asked me to go home. My mother was trying to arrange a marriage with a Chinese girl. She had catalogues, pictures of girls with their age and height. All the communities were the same, they wanted to keep their marriages within the community. Why do you think the Irish built that rec centre behind St. Brigid's?

"We lived upstairs in the Chinese Nationalist Party building on Saint-Vallier. It was a political movement that supported Chang Kai-shek, and my father was the president. People would meet there to exchange news about China, and it was a sort of mutual aid society. They even had their own bank. I remember the men playing mahjong and gambling there. I heard of people losing tens of thousands of dollars, or their restaurants.

"Saint-Vallier was Chinese, and we spoke English. We would walk to St. Patrick's School together in the morning in a group. There were some nuns who had been in China and they took us under their wing, so we became Catholics, but we kept our Buddhist traditions too. We used to have our ceremonies in the St. Charles Graveyard, bringing food for the ancestors in the Buddhist way. We also celebrated the New Moon Festival and the Chinese New Year. The last parade was about 15 years ago. When they knocked down our houses to build the overpasses everyone moved away. So many moved to Charlesbourg that they called 41st and 42nd Avenue 'Rues des Chinois.'

"When the language laws came along I didn't mind. I felt worse for the francophones; they didn't have the choice any more. I have more rights than they do now."

Napoleon Woo

Chinese Parade, 1945.

Knitting the balaclavas again

World War II

During World War II the issue of conscription again caused a rift between Quebec City's English- and French-speaking communities, with many French Canadians again objecting to being forced to fight a distant European war, while British-origin Quebec City teenagers lied shamelessly about their age in their haste to join up. More than 1,400 boys from the two English high schools in town, the High School of Quebec and St. Patrick's, signed up to go to war. Ronald Blair remembers:

> Lots of the men I worked with in the woods were there to avoid conscription. They didn't have to go overseas, but they were against the war anyway. Why should they sacrifice their lives for a quarrel over in Europe? I was contemptuous at the time. It never occurred to me not to join up. Nearly all the French Canadians at the High School joined up too. I looked forward to going to war, and I was disappointed that the war ended before I went overseas. Both my brothers went: one was the mine disposal officer for the west coast of Scotland; the other was a tail-gunner in the Air Force. Both survived, but many of my friends died in the war. When we read the list of them on Remembrance Day at the Cathedral, I still cry. I knew every single one of them.

Anglophones volunteered in the war efforts of the YMCA, the Knights of Columbus, the Navy League and the Girl Guides Association. Many women joined the patriotic Imperial Order Daughters of the Empire, knitting socks and balaclavas for soldiers. Some joined the Red Cross Women's Work Committee, which looked after the families of the men gone to war. They opened a tea shop called La Bonne Salade on St. Louis Street, with the proceeds going towards buying an ambulance for the troops overseas. Red Cross women also made crepe paper violets which they sold in the churches, at the Château Frontenac and to visitors passing through the train station.

The heroic stories reported back home did not always match up with the realities of the front. Evoy Delaney was a young Quebec City Irishman who fought in Europe. Emerging full of shrapnel from a weekend of bitter and vicious fighting in Belgium, he was asked by a reporter what it was like. Almost speechless with horror, all he could say was "Jesus *Christ!*" The imaginative reporter wrote that Delaney had replied, "We're there to represent our country. It was tough, but we can handle 'em!"

Homecoming, October 1945.

After finishing grade 11, 16-year-old Irish Quebecer Kenneth Cambon left his job in a soda fountain to enlist in the Royal Rifles of Canada, a Quebec City regiment. The regiment was sent to Hong Kong in 1941 under the command of Quebec City lawyer Lieutenant-Colonel W.J. Home. Along with a Winnipeg regiment and four regiments from India and Britain, they were meant to prevent a Japanese invasion. They didn't have a hope. Kenneth Cambon returned in 1945 to tell the tale, but 290 Canadians were killed in the battle and another 264 died during the four years in forced labour and prison camps.

The war turned Quebec City into a garrison town once more: 14,000 people were employed in the munitions industry, 7,000 of them in the St. Malo area alone. Anglophones got work teaching French-Canadian airmen, the Royal Canadian Air Force in its wisdom having chosen Quebec City as the ideal place for its men to learn English. Once the war was over, with most of the arms industries dismantled and the Canadian National Railways having closed their shops, postwar unemployment (9%) was the worst in any Canadian city. However, the city soon returned briefly to its old status as part of the economic heart of the continent. Inspired by Industrial Commissioner Armand Viau, the municipality bought the vacant St. Malo land in 1945 and resold it to European and American companies such as General Electric and Goodyear. By 1954, 40 new companies had set up shop in Quebec City, most of them in the St. Malo industrial zone.

Many of the specialists and managers of these new companies were brought in from elsewhere, and most were anglophone. Between 1941 and 1951 the Protestant population increased by 10%, and in 1952 alone the city's Protestant schools grew by 18%. The old anglophone-controlled power monopolies, however, saw their hold broken in 1944 when Premier Adélard Godbout's government bought 27 electricity companies, mostly owned by English speakers, and created Hydro-Quebec.

Canadian Tribal Destroyers in Action, Commander Anthony Law, 1946.

Anthony Law was born in England to Canadian parents, and returned to Quebec City in 1917. He studied under Fred Varley and Percyval Tudor-Hart, and during the war was commissioned as an official naval war artist. "I remember a certain night when we met a large enemy convoy, heavily escorted," he said during an interview with the *Quebec Chronicle-Telegraph* in 1943. "They put twelve star shells into the sky ... That was the subject of my painting showing our boats in the middle of the night, with all the details shown because of the brilliant light coming from the star shells."

It was under Godbout, too, that women finally broke men's exclusive hold on Quebec politics. Anglophone women had been taking business courses and working as secretaries and bank tellers since early in the century. Journalist Gerry Burridge, the daughter of an icebreaker captain, had graduated from a commercial course in 1924 and got a job at the Bank of Commerce for $10 a week. Although in some milieus there was still a social stigma attached to working women, in wartime they took over many jobs previously done by men, proving that they were equally capable and that the world held together even if they left the kitchen sink during working hours. Montreal women marched to Quebec City 14 times from 1922 to 1940 to put the case for women's suffrage before the premier. They finally went to the polls for the first time in 1944. But it wasn't until 20 years later that they could sign a contract, or sue somebody.

"Quebec woman, denied the vote, hears the news from benighted Turkey," Arthur George Racey, n.d.

Here Quebec City cartoonist Arthur Racey captures the irony of the fact that while women in backward or "benighted" Turkey were able to vote by 1930, Quebec women were still waiting to be able to vote in provincial elections, and would have to keep waiting until 1944.

Regina Rosenhek presenting social work award to Mary Robinson, Quebec chapter of the National Council of Jewish Women, 1953.

Jewish women in the 1950s were still looking after starving European war survivors showing up in Quebec City. Hungarian refugees arriving in 1956–57 were greeted by Quebec's Jewish women's organizations, including the Quebec chapter of the National Council of Jewish Women of Canada, Hebrew Ladies' Aid and the synagogue Sisterhood. Regina Rosenhek, president of the Sisterhood, recalls: "The rabbi called me and said, 'Regina, there's a boatload of Jewish people coming in, and they haven't had a kosher meal for months.' We bought 300 pounds of meat from Weisberg's, brisket and tongue, and cooked it all up into Jewish dishes. We got the men to take the food down, and although there were other denominations on board, at the smell of it alone everyone suddenly turned Jewish. They almost had a riot."

Chatting on the phone

Duplessis and the anglophones

Much of the expansion of Quebec industries of this period was due to Maurice Duplessis, leader of the Union Nationale party and premier from 1936 to 1939, and then again from 1944 to 1959. Some anglophones saw Duplessis as reactionary, authoritarian and only a step removed from Hitler. But Duplessis left English-speaking businesses and institutions, such as the Protestant school board and the Jeffery Hale Hospital, largely intact. Instead of using the few anglophone ministers in his government as intermediaries, he dealt with leaders of these institutions directly on the phone or in person. Many of Quebec City's anglophones fell for his charm and voted him repeatedly back into office, even though his expanding civil service excluded anglophones almost entirely.

Duplessis indirectly increased the English-speaking population of Quebec City by inviting American capital and businesses to Quebec. His strongly anti-union stance and a vast pool of cheap labour, mostly from the Irish and francophone communities, made American companies glad to come. It didn't seem to bother Duplessis that anglophones kept all the best jobs.

While some of the newcomers joined the older English-speaking families in Montcalmville, others began inhabiting a new form of suburb, the "bedroom community." They formed a close community, with their own churches and sports clubs, and if they chose to they could shop almost exclusively in English. There was Baller's Grocery and Kinnear's drugstore on Cartier. There was Herman Young's hardware store, Moore's stationery, and McKenna's the florist. They could buy clothes at Holt Renfrew or at Gardner's, the Jewish tailor, shoes from Gale or a watch from Hatch or Birks. Some of the newcomers never learned French.

Anglophone shopping: Simons' department store on Fabrique Street, 1967, and Pollack's on Charest Boulevard.

New anglophone arrivals in Quebec could go shopping in stores that were run by English-speaking families that had been around for generations, such as Pollack and Simons. Son of a Scottish sailmaker who had settled in Lac Beauport, John Simons opened his first store in 1840. It moved to Fabrique Street in 1870, and in 1961 expanded to the shopping centre. Maurice Pollack's new department store on Boulevard Charest, built in 1950, was the most modern in the city, while the city's first multistorey car park, across the road, was recalled by one anglophone shopper as "the coldest and most miserable building in Quebec."

For sports, they could join the Quebec Swimming and Athletic Club, the YWCA or the Victoria Curling Club, where membership for some, such as Hugh Bignell, was a family affair going down generations. "They had a competition every year called the Medal Shots," he said, "and the winner won a long gold chain with a list of all the previous winners. When I won it in 1960s, I saw that my father had won it in the 1930s, and my grandfather had won it in the early 1900s."Although the Quebec snowshoe clubs had gone out of fashion by the 1940s, some of the favourite anglophone sporting traditions, such as hunting and fishing, continued unabated.

Women and girls at the Young Women's Christian Association (YWCA), W.B. Edwards, 1931.

Straying from its original mandate to help immigrant women avoid prostitution, poverty and drink, in 1916 the YWCA opened the Douglas Hall swimming pool and gym on St. Ursula Street. Swimmers had to take a medical exam before entering the water, as polio was rife. Religious authorities were scandalized: all these naked bodies were occasions for sin. In the 1930s the pool became famous for synchronized swimming, and by 1950 the swimming instructor, Suzanne Éon, was attracting students from all over the world. The team won a silver medal at the Pan American Games in 1971.

Greater yellow-legs
The hunter-conservationists

Early in the century keen sportsmen were increasingly disturbed by the wholesale destruction of the fish and wildlife of the St. Lawrence Valley, where dynamite fishermen and avid nest-raiders were hand in glove with government game wardens, and even went hunting together. The Provancher Society, still going strong to this day, was founded in 1919 to reverse this "destructive mentality" through education and the acquisition of land for reserves. Its motto was *J'aime, j'instruis, je protège* (I love, I teach, I protect). The society was bilingual, and alternated francophone and anglophone presidents. It successfully lobbied the government for better game laws and enforcement and the establishment of a marine biology station, and acquired two islands in the river as bird sanctuaries. But its main focus was education, to which it devoted 70% of its budget. School children could be members for 10 cents a year, and the society's lectures at the Château Frontenac were popular events. Each lecture began with a piano concert or a short film, followed by a guest presenter. One of the presenters was Grey Owl. An Englishman by birth whose real name was Archibald Stansfield Belaney, Grey Owl claimed to be half Apache and, thanks to the prompting of his Iroquois wife Anahareo, was a pioneer conservationist.

Knowing the land as intimately as they did, keen hunters were often also the keenest conservationists, and worked hard to preserve the wilderness. One of the mainstays of the Provancher Society was Rex Meredith, a notary and an avid hunter. He received his first gun when he was 13, and for 60 years he went shooting several times a week each fall from September 1 to early December, covering hundreds of kilometres on foot up and down the St. Lawrence. He loved hunting snipe best of all. He and his friends averaged about 400 per season, but scored an all-time high of 938 in the fall of 1934. He also hunted various kinds of plover, greater yellow-legs, partridge, hare and bufflehead ducks. One of his favourite hunting companions was Elizabeth Petry, also an expert hunter who shot bear, moose, fox, deer, hare, common snipe, Jack snipe, black duck, teal, pintail, Canada geese and snow geese. In 1956 Meredith counted up all the snipe he and his friends had shot since 1911: the total was 12,672. "We ought to be ashamed of ourselves," he wrote, "but we aren't." They may have put a small dent in the snipe population, but the paving over of Quebec's marshes, first by Anglo-Canadian in 1928 and then by the Autoroute Dufferin-Montmorency in 1968, eliminated Quebec's snipe once and for all.

Many hunting and fishing clubs took over land that had been First Nations hunting territory, and depended on the Aboriginal population to act as guides. The Grand Chief of the Huron, Max Gros-Louis, reflected, "When I was 14, I worked as a guide at the Triton Club, one of the best hunting and fishing clubs in Canada. I found some of my grandfather's old traps around the portages. But I was already resigned to the fact that we couldn't hunt there any more. We were afraid of the provincial game wardens, and the guardians, and of jail. They would arrest you if they caught you hunting or fishing or trapping. When the Parti Québécois took power, they abolished all the clubs, but they forgot to protect the game. The clubs didn't respect our rights, but they were much better for the game."

Grey Owl, writer and conservationist (1888–1938), ca. 1930.

A.C.M. Thomson and Rex Meredith hunting on the Beauport Flats, ca. 1950.

Max Gros-Louis, future Grand Chief of the Huron, Rivière Huron, 1953.

St. Patrick's Day

Keeping the culture

The traditional St. Patrick's Day parades came to an end in 1926, but the day's cultural celebrations continued. Local talent prepared months ahead of time for the much-anticipated soirées at the Capitol Theatre (and later the Palais Montcalm), featuring everything from poetry, plays and symphonies to club-swinging demonstrations and clog dances. More solemn celebrations took place at High Mass on the same day, when a sacred and patriotic repertoire involved the city's most talented classical musicians.

Irish Quebecers had long demanded their own Catholic anglophone institutions, but they still found themselves between a rock and a hard place. As the province did not provide for matriculation courses or exams, St. Patrick's High School used the Protestant exams set by McGill until 1939, when the government set up its own High School Leaving examinations. Religious orders dominated education for both anglophone and francophone Catholics until the late 1960s: 90% of the teachers at St. Patrick's and Leonard School were still either Christian Brothers or Sisters of Charity until 1965.

The establishment of the Leonard School for Irish girls in 1935, run by the Halifax Sisters of Charity, was strongly opposed by both the Catholic school board and Mayor Grégoire, who saw yet another separate school for the Irish as taking away money from the French system. A civic election was fought on this issue, and Grégoire was overthrown. Irish girls, scattered in 13 schools across the city, assembled for the first time at their new school in 1939.

When St. Patrick's school moved from McMahon Street to de Salaberry in 1918, it was following a general westward migration of the Irish from their old downtown cold-water flats in the Saint-Louis and Saint-Jean-Baptiste neighbourhoods to Montcalm. The Irish remnant in the old neighbourhood was abruptly erased in 1969, when 1,239 houses on 21 hectares in the Irish quarter were demolished for the new Cité Parlementaire and Saint-Cyrille (René-Lévesque) and Dufferin (Honoré-Mercier) boulevards. By that time the new Irish centre of operations was around de Salaberry and de Maisonneuve.

Delivery from Boswell's Breweries to the Irish tavern "Chien d'Or Café," Rue du Fort, ca. 1917.

On St. Patrick's Night a large contingent repaired to the Chien d'Or, a favourite Irish venue for singing, telling stories, reciting poetry and, once in a while, fighting. "The floors were wooden, they gave a bit," said proprietor Bill Noonan of the 1920s. "Now they're tile, and if your head hits that, there's no give." For a long time, full-blooded Catholic Irishness was a condition of entry on St. Patrick's Day. "If a Protestant came in these doors, they'd kill him," said Noonan. Even an Irishman with a French name would be challenged: "He'd say his mother was Irish, but there'd still be a fight."

After the war the Irish were swept up in the ubiquitous suburban drift and dispersed beyond the city limits. English Catholic public elementary schools were built in Sillery (St. Stephen's) and Sainte-Foy (St. Vincent's), and the American Catholic Marymount sisters moved their college on Rue Mont-Carmel, in the old city, out to Sillery. St. Patrick's was no longer a neighbourhood school but became a gathering point for the diaspora. It was also no longer a boys' school (it began taking girls in 1956), nor an exclusively Irish school. It educated Huron children from Lorette and non-Irish children of Catholic immigrants, such as several families from Italy and Greece. Irish sisters with a history of missions in China ensured the enrolment of several Chinese immigrant children at St. Patrick's, and in Sillery the American Marymount sisters enrolled Jewish children in their Catholic college. When it came to sports, the rivalry between the Catholic and Protestant high schools was intense – until it came to a match with a French school, in which case there was a seamless solidarity among all anglophones.

Irish anglophones in Quebec City were in danger of losing their cohesion as a group, and not just because of the individualism in an increasingly consumer-oriented society. People with Irish names were by now just as likely to be francophone, and the anglophone Irish who had intermarried with non-Irish anglophones now stood out less as a group than earlier. But a strong Irish Quebec contingent, including Father Tom O'Grady, the only anglophone diocesan priest in the city, refused to watch the distinctive Irish-Quebec culture blend into the scenery. They wanted Irish youth to be able to get a BA, in English, in a Catholic institution in Quebec City.

Aerial view of Cité Parlementaire before reconstruction, ca. 1965.
Faubourg Saint-Louis and Faubourg Saint-Jean, in the foreground of this picture, were where Quebec's Irish population once lived. The area is now a complex of hotels, financial institutions, government high-rises, office blocks, a shopping centre and a conference centre. This massive reconstruction began in 1965 with the demolition of three hectares of houses to broaden Boulevard Saint-Cyrille (now Boulevard René-Levesque), shown here cutting the first swath through the neighbourhood. By 1978, 50 residential blocks had been demolished, covering 21 hectares of the city.

Cardinal Maurice Roy agreed with O'Grady that there was a need for more Quebec City–trained anglophone priests, which would require streaming Irish boys into the seminary. The diocese would underwrite the venture, and since the newly built Grand Séminaire (which now houses the Archives Nationales du Québec among other things) had only attracted a handful of novices instead of the hundreds it was designed for, in 1958 most of an entire wing was given over to the new college. It was named after the only Celtic saint to have been duly canonized by Rome, St. Lawrence O'Toole, Abbot of Glendalough.

St. Lawrence College, founded in 1958, was modelled on the classical college system (private colleges for francophones, at one time the only secondary schools available to francophone Catholics) and affiliated with Laval University. Anglophone Catholic boys no longer had to go to Nova Scotia (St. Francis Xavier in Antigonish), Prince Edward Island (St. Dunstan's) or Montreal (Loyola) for a degree: a BA from St. Lawrence gave them access to advanced study at Laval University. The college soon developed an active extension department through which adults could gain degrees, offering a series of "Green Lectures" and producing a regular TV show on CKMI called "Celtic Cameos," highlighting the Irish contribution to Quebec history.

But no sooner had the first few batches of boys received their BAs when reforms following the Parent Report on education ended the classical college system in 1967, as part of a generalized removal of education from the control of the Catholic Church. The college had turned out only one priest, who had become a Jesuit. The Catholic diocese promptly put the college building up for sale. Before sweeping away in his black Chevrolet for the last time, the rector, Father Philip Mifflin, handed the keys to a new lay director, Edward Murphy, along with the advice to "keep control of hiring teachers, and don't lose your temper."

The entry of St. Lawrence into the secular CEGEP system (intermediary colleges between high school and university in Quebec) was deeply symbolic of the transition between the old anglophone Quebec City and the new. The old anglophone solitudes were breached, and St. Lawrence CEGEP created a linguistic community instead of an ethnic or religious one. For many francophone students, too, this was their first contact with anglophones.

To some, though, it seemed the Irish in Quebec City had only just managed to secure their own institutions when they now had to fight to preserve them. Even the celebrated soirées at Palais Montcalm were discontinued in 1965. They were henceforth held on a smaller scale in the schools and in St. Brigid's Home. Reacting to the loss of such a rich communal heritage, the Irish were the first Quebec City anglophones to dig deeply into their own roots as a community. In 1973, Larkin Kerwin, Marianna O'Gallagher and Harry Hannon formed the Irish Heritage Society, and undertook the first study of Irish marriages in Quebec City from 1760 onwards.

Dr. Larkin Kerwin (1924–2004).
Dr. Larkin Kerwin was the first lay rector of Laval University (1972–77). "A boy from St. Patrick's School becoming rector of Laval epitomizes the reality of being English-speaking in Quebec City – of how the two communities are meshed," said his daughter Lupita. He was instrumental in the establishment of St. Lawrence College. World-renowned atomic and molecular physicist, Dr. Kerwin was president of the National Research Council for ten years and president of the Canadian Space Agency from 1989 to 1992. A Companion of the Order of Canada and an Officer of l'Ordre National du Québec, he was awarded 15 honorary degrees from Canadian universities. He died in 2004.

St. Lawrence College.

Following the Parent Report on education, the government ended the private classical colleges in Quebec, including St. Lawrence College, and instead established public CEGEPs (*collèges d'enseignement général et professionnel*) in 1967. The government did not support an English CEGEP in the city, so the new lay director of St. Lawrence College, Edward Murphy, was faced with having to find both an affiliation and a building. The college affiliated with Champlain Regional College in 1971 and moved into Laurier Lanes, an old bowling alley where Place de la Cité is now. The college came to rest in its current quarters in Sainte-Foy in 1977.

Living Witness

Patrick McKenna's great-grandfather came to Quebec City in 1848 and was assistant emigrant agent under Alexander Buchanan (see Volume I, p. 104). His family have been parishioners at St. Patrick's for several generations, moving with the church from the McMahon Street area to the Irish neighbourhood that grew up around de Salaberry, where St. Patrick's school and church are to this day. He taught at St. Patrick's High School for 32 years, including 13 as principal.

"As a child I lived on Scott Street, near the Parliament buildings, the part of the street now called Rue de l'Amérique-Française. But before they tore it down, it was an Irish neighbourhood: Plessis Street, d'Artigny, St. Michael's Street, St. Patrick's Street. I used to skate over to St. Pat's on Saturday morning, on the streets all the way, and spend the day on the rink.

"My father worked at the personnel office for Anglo-Canadian Pulp, looking after the welfare of all the employees. He looked after maybe 2,000 employees. If you were a Catholic it was very difficult to break through. The word was that you had to be a Freemason in order to get a promotion. I worked at Anglo for five summers, and Dad got me work through Sarsfield Quinn, the only Catholic that really had a position of authority there. I worked in the yard, on the upkeep of the railroads and in the greenhouse.

"My grandmother, Cecilia Duffy, was born at sea in 1857, and baptized at Grosse Île. The Irish used to be very traditionalist. My grandmother was very strict about marriage, for example. She had five daughters and she didn't really want them to marry at all, but worst of all, the first one married a French-speaking person. She wouldn't see her after that, although she adored her grandchildren.

My father married a French woman too, and it took a few years before she accepted her. But she had unshakable faith, and that was an inspiration to the family. She always supported the church, and helped organize fundraisers for St. Brigid's Asylum.

"People talk about the two solitudes, referring to the French and the English, but the English and the Irish were two solitudes too. We hardly ever saw each other. There was no common meeting place except the Garrison Club, but you had to have money for that. Our social life was St. Patrick's Church, the school and sporting events. The YMCA too was known to be more Protestant until the 1970s, although the Catholic girls at the Leonard School used to take the synchronized swimming classes at the YWCA in the 1950s. Both communities had very strong traditions. Now I see people from very different traditions working together, but that was missing back then. You don't have to give up what you have to work closely together. Now I meet other English speakers from Quebec and I never saw them in my life. We've lived here for years, and yet never crossed paths in this small community.

"Even before Bill 101, there were lots of kids at St. Patrick's High School whose mother tongue was French, and a lot of French was spoken in the school. It's a difficult issue – the parishioners would come and see me on Sunday and complain that all they heard at the school was French, and it wasn't like that before, in the 40s and 50s. I'd say, you should thank the Lord they are perfectly bilingual. It was always a struggle to get them to speak English all the time. If they don't use it in school, where will they use it?"

Patrick McKenna

Suburban solitudes

The new exodus

When the Noonan brothers of the Chien d'Or moved their operations to Sainte-Foy, they were only following their clients. English speakers were moving out of downtown enclaves into suburbs, or "bedroom" communities. Instead of shopping from store to store, department stores such as Kresge's, Paquet's and Pollack's were the rage, and for food shopping it was A&P and Steinberg's. Ready-to-wear clothes appeared, and for the first time many women began to buy clothes instead of making them. The first shopping centre, Place Sainte-Foy, opened in 1957.

Life for married women shifted dramatically: the "feminine mystique," as Betty Friedan called it, required the suburban wife to be passionately interested in makeup, clothes, shopping, interior decorating and being ready for her husband at 5:30 pm, wearing a silk negligée and with cocktail in hand. With the baby boom in full swing, however, the image in the women's magazines was far from the reality, which was a houseful of tiny children and chronic exhaustion. The old supports of neighbourhood and extended family had disappeared forever, and for many anglophones new to the community, the suburbs were lonely places.

One aspect of modern life, though, did alleviate the loneliness: radio. People lucky enough to own radio sets had been listening to the radio in both languages since 1922, when English-language CFCF and French-language CKAC shared a studio in Montreal. In 1933, the Canadian Radio Broadcasting Commission set up the bilingual station CRCK in Quebec City. The Commission was replaced three years later by the new Canadian Broadcasting Corporation, which began broadcasting from the Château Frontenac as CBV. Women rearranged their domestic lives around radio, changing meal times or staying home especially to tune into the CBV broadcast of the Metropolitan Opera and the BBC News as well as local news, sports and theatre in both English and French.

Maison Chevalier, Barbara O'Halloran.

While anglophone women may have revelled in shopping at the new malls, listening to the new radios and stacking their dishes in the new dishwashers, some were also gifted artists and writers. They hastened to record Quebec's quickly disappearing architectural heritage before the lust for concrete had its wicked way. Artist Barbara O'Halloran (1907-1996) studied alongside Albert Rousseau and Simone Hudon at the École des Beaux-Arts on Rue Saint-Joachim under Ivan Neilson, and later under Francesco Iacurto. She illustrated books by Quebec City author Blodwen Davies, and held several exhibitions. Her paintings and etchings are still scattered throughout the houses of many of Quebec City's English-speaking families.

Montcalm Market, Valentine & Sons Publishing Co., ca. 1912.

Place Laurier, ca. 1965.

The car replaces the horse-drawn wagon, the parking lot replaces the hitching rail, the shopping cart replaces the wicker basket, fluorescent lights replace the open sky, and fast food replaces fresh snacks from street vendors' stalls. Shopping centres spread throughout North America in the postwar period. Quebec City, which once had eight markets, succumbed with Place Sainte-Foy in 1957. The Montcalm Market in Place d'Youville lasted until 1931, when the market hall was demolished, while the St. Roch market at Pointe-aux-Lièvres held on until 1977.

A private station, originally opened in 1949, gained unprecedented success in the 1960s when it dropped its CBC content to 20%, added pop music and went bilingual. However, federal regulators consistently opposed its bilingualism and its low level of CBC content and, ignoring petitions signed by many angry young Quebecers, closed the station down in 1975.

When suburban housewives saw in the 1950s that women journalists, radio and TV hosts were now discussing topics that used to be the preserve of men (politics! psychology! literature!), some of them asked themselves, why not me? Their voices began to be heard on the city's radio and TV stations, and other women joined the University Women's Club of Quebec (founded 1937) to discuss girls' education, foreign policy and suffrage, discussions that had hitherto been held only in male camera and wreathed in cigar smoke.

Radio.

In 1949 Joseph-Narcisse Thivierge founded the English radio station CJNT (largely music) on Rue des Jardins. Norman Lucas took over with CFOM in 1967, with a mandate to broadcast CBC's English-language programs to Quebec City and slot in a few extra hours of local programming. It repeatedly petitioned Ottawa to be permitted to broadcast in both languages, but to no avail. The station struggled along until it lowered its CBC content to 20%, began broadcasting pop music and added French to English. Francophone youth tuned in too, listenership shot from 16,000 to 110,000, and it was ordered off the air in 1975.

Cultural starvation
University Women's Club of Quebec

In 1937 a club was founded to enable women to "socialize in an intellectual way" and study public affairs. They began by inviting speakers to inform them about the need for juvenile courts, or about the Grenfell medical mission in Newfoundland, but soon moved to political advocacy by protesting both Duplessis's Padlock Law and the lack of opportunities for Quebec women in the civil service.

World War II pitched the club into the war effort, and it raised money for refugees and found homes for children evacuated from Britain. Two members were appointed to the regional council of the Wartime Prices and Trade Board. By the time the war ended the club had invited francophone members to join. Alternating speakers in French and English were invited, an effort that ended a few years later because "although a few French members came to hear the English speakers, no English members came to hear the French speakers." Some of the francophone members ended up forming their own Femmes Universitaires. Numbers waned after the war, and Mrs. Lagloire pronounced the hope that with the return of normal conditions after the war and the reavailability of domestic help, members would have more freedom to devote to their tasks as leaders.

The club was actively involved in the arts, urging the creation of the Canada Council in 1952. From 1955 onwards the club rented the Palais Montcalm or the Institut Canadien and sponsored a prominent national touring theatre company, Canadian Players, to bring plays by Shakespeare, George Bernard Shaw, Oscar Wilde and Bertolt Brecht to "culture-starved" English Quebec City, with all profits going to bursaries. It also supported English libraries and put on art exhibitions, plays and concerts by local artists at the Palais Montcalm and Laval University.

Political involvement continued into the 1970s. In 1967, members invited Eric Kierans to speak to the club about Canada's monetary policy. The club prepared a brief for the Gendron Commission on the French language (1969), held a public meeting on the Status of Women Report (1970), and in 1973 welcomed René Lévesque as a speaker.

In 1974 it began holding an annual book sale to raise money for study bursaries. These sales, through which the English-speaking community effects a massive exchange of precious reading matter in English, have now been an annual event for 30 years.

Fighting words

English television

Barbara Smith and Rosemary Cannon were both young Quebec City anglophone women who penetrated the wreaths of cigar smoke when they were suddenly catapulted to the centre of media attention with the advent of television. Barbara Smith was 18 when, according to George Lovett, manager at Quebec City's new CKMI-TV, he plucked her out of a chair in the lobby where she was waiting for a friend and escorted her swiftly into the host's seat for *Dateline*, the station's afternoon current affairs program, because he thought "her voice was so good." She went on to anchor CBC radio's major national newscast.

Anglophones had a choice of two TV stations in Quebec City in the late 1950s, one in French (CFCM) and one in English (CKMI), and they watched both. The stations operated out of the same building on Myrand Avenue, and viewers sometimes saw the same characters appearing on both channels. One of CKMI's creations, the immensely popular *Teen Club* with host Norm Wright, is still remembered by many Quebecers of both languages today. Inspired by Dick Clark's *American Bandstand*, it featured young American and Canadian pop singers, interspersed with interviews with local anglophone high school students about youth issues. It was soon copied by CFCM.

CKMI was owned by an American company, Famous Players, and the station ran American films and a late-night talk show that largely featured Hollywood stars. About 60% of its programming was fed by CBC, but the local programming was unique. One day when host Rosemary Cannon's guests didn't show up during a snowstorm, she began playing a rubber of bridge on air with the staff. It was such a hit that she had calls begging her to make it a regular feature. Francophones from its sister station collaborated in *Biting Words*, a comedy show that spoofed the CBC's intellectual *Fighting Words*. In 1970, when the CRTC ended outright American ownership of Canadian media, the station was sold to a Montreal company, and the local programming dwindled.

Although the current television and radio fare, Global TV and the CBC's Quebec Community Network, cover some local anglophone news, they have never quite filled the vacuum left by Quebec City's unique brand of local bilingual media.

University Women's Club of Quebec members, ca. 1945.

Erasing the roses

Nationalism and the Quiet Revolution

Francophones were getting fed up. The church seemed to control most aspects of life, and English speakers controlled whatever was left. English signs were prominent: a survey in 1933 of two of the city's main roads found English on more than half the signs, even though anglophones made up only 7% of the regional population. Nationalist elements in the church, press and Chamber of Commerce wanted to *franciser* the city's architecture and deplored anything that was reminiscent of the British regime, by now the origin of 90% of the buildings left in the Old City.

The movement to rebuild the capital as reflecting its French rather than its British past took architectural form under Louis-Alexandre Taschereau's government (1920–36) in a multitude of public buildings in the Paris Beaux-Arts style. Place Royale was seen as the cradle of French civilization in North America, and beginning with the Maison Chevalier in 1956, it was rebuilt in an exclusively New France style which, according to historian Jean-Marie Lebel, "aimed more at presenting a glorious image of the French past than at historical accuracy."

Parliamentary structures and appointments reflected a distaste for remnants of the British regime. The important post of treasurer, which had been held by an anglophone since 1867, passed to French speakers when Maurice Duplessis was returned to power in 1944, while the token anglophone was given the mines portfolio. The fleur-de-lis replaced the British flag flying over Parliament. When residents suggested that a quarter of the fleur-de-lis flag be devoted to a symbol depicting an English-speaking culture, such as a thistle or a rose, the idea was rejected. Spencer Wood was renamed the Bois de Coulonge, and Lieutenant Governor Paul Comtois died when the house burned down in 1966.

Cataraqui.

The age of the anglophone villas was finally over when Catherine (Rhodes) Tudor-Hart, the last resident of Cataraqui, died in 1972. Her executors tried to sell the house to the government, but there was no enthusiasm. Paintings and furniture from all over Europe were briskly auctioned off: *Le Soleil* declared there was *rien de bien québécois* (nothing really Québécois). In 1975 the city bought the house to save the property from developers, but no alternative plans bore fruit. A pack of wild dogs moved into the leaky and rotting house, so that even children were afraid to come and play in it. Finally it was saved by the women of Sillery: Andrée Garneau Dorion, Margaret Delisle and the Bagatelle Foundation. Cataraqui has belonged to the Commission de la capitale nationale du Québec since 2002.

After Duplessis's death in 1959, the vise-like grip of the Catholic Church and of anglophone businesses began to loosen. When the Liberals defeated the Union Nationale in the 1960 election, the new premier, Jean Lesage, announced that the Great Darkness was over, and that from now on Quebecers would be Masters in Their Own House (*Maîtres chez nous*). Massive reforms were undertaken in the areas of education, women's rights and nationalization of industry. Hippies, divorce, abortion, homosexuality and the Pill were suddenly on centre stage, and it seemed that, overnight, Quebec society left behind the church and its respect for the status quo, and entered the modern world.

The Liberals lost the 1966 election, and René Lévesque, who had been part of Lesage's *équipe du tonnerre*, left the party in 1967 and formed the separatist Parti Québécois a year later, making it clear that he thought Quebec's relationship with Canada was like a bad marriage and would end in divorce: "If both are able to sleep in the same bed, then, fine, it can bring good results. But if they are unable, then they should sleep in different rooms."

Changes in traditional institutions, rituals and nomenclature accelerated: the "speech from the throne" became the "inaugural speech" and the Legislative Assembly became the National Assembly. The unelected Legislative Council or "Upper House" (retained in 1867 only in Quebec so as to protect the English-speaking minority from possible abuses by the French-speaking majority) was abolished, and its chamber, the *Salon Rouge*, became

a committee room. While English speakers had made up nearly half the cabinet in the 1890s, when the Parti Québécois was elected in 1976 English speakers for the first time were completely excluded from cabinet. Research priorities were changing too: as part of the process of identity recovery, those that emphasized Quebec's francophone history now got the lion's share of university funding.

In 1963 the Wolfe monument and the statue of Queen Victoria in Victoria Park were blown up by the terrorist Front de Libération du Québec (FLQ). The FLQ set six bombs in Sainte-Foy. But it staged its most spectacular coup in Montreal in 1970, kidnapping British trade commissioner James Richard Cross and Quebec cabinet minister Pierre Laporte. After Laporte was murdered, much of the sympathy for the FLQ among francophones melted away. The War Measures Act had been invoked, and within two days police made 1,628 raids. Tommy Douglas of the NDP called it using a "sledgehammer to crack a peanut." The FLQ turned out to have consisted of about 35 people. The FLQ may have been the extremist end of a much quieter revolution, but it had its impact on anglophones. Somewhat to their surprise, they found themselves the object of deep-seated and sometimes violent resentment.

Throne Speech in the Legislative Council Chamber or *Salon Rouge*, W.B. Edwards, 1925.
Parliament in Quebec was "Westminster in miniature," according to historian Damase Potvin. From the fur hat with ostrich plumes worn by the lieutenant governor when reading the Speech from the Throne down to a legendary snuffbox on the clerk's table, a gift from the Lord Mayor of London, British traditions were zealously maintained until the 1970s. The walls of the Legislative Council (Upper House) chamber were red, like the House of Lords, and like the House of Commons, those of the Lower House were green (the colour of cheap woad) until 1978, when they were painted blue. Speeches, however, were always in both languages.

In 1971 the government took over health and social services, and the church ladies and religious orders had to hang up their hats and veils and retire into the background of social welfare works. Although most English speakers were glad overall that the church had lost its grip, many felt that now the state had simply replaced the church in this particular nation's bedroom. They were also afraid that Quebec nationalism was an ethnically defined project that excluded anyone whose ancestry was not French, and many felt increasingly unwelcome as legislative restrictions limited the use of their language.

George Marler, Hervé Mageau, ca. 1960.
The last of the influential anglophone spokesmen for business in cabinet was George Marler. A prominent member of the Liberal caucus while in opposition, and briefly the leader, he was appointed to the Legislative Council and to the cabinet as minister without portfolio when the Liberals took office in 1960. The descendant of an 18th-century French Anglican minister in Quebec City, he spoke perfect French: his successor as Liberal leader, Georges-Émile Lapalme, claimed that Marler only made one mistake between 1950 and 1954, which was a "possible failure to use the subjunctive."

General de Gaulle's visit, Magella Chouinard, 1967.
"France hails the advent of a people" said French President Charles de Gaulle to the crowds outside City Hall in 1967, "who wishes in every domain to take its destiny into its own hands." Journalist Hubert Bauch from the *Quebec Chronicle-Telegraph* recalled, "I was 20 years old at the time. The crowds were huge, he gave this very nationalist speech and I said to myself, My God, he's going to say it! And he didn't, but he said it ["*Vive le Québec libre!*"] the next day in Montreal. They put on a terrific meal afterwards – that was the first time I got drunk on champagne."

Changing tunes

The royal visits

One area in which French-speaking Quebecers expressed their attitude to everything British was their response to royal visits. King George VI and Queen Elizabeth visited Quebec in the spring of 1939, hoping to drum up Canadian support for the looming war against Hitler. Historian Gustave Lanctot observed:

An afternoon drive brought the King and Queen to the Battlefields Park, where more than sixty thousand persons were assembled in the grand setting of the Plains overlooking the river and the Laurentides. Soon silence prevailed, and twenty-five thousand voices of schoolchildren, fervid and youthful, sang *Dieu sauve le roi* and *Ô Canada*, with a stirring crescendo that made nerves and hearts tingle with emotion. It was Quebec at its best. So was it also in the evening, when at the banquet given at the Château Frontenac by Premier Duplessis and his Government, Their Majesties on leaving were greeted by a spontaneous ovation.

Next morning (May 18), the King and Queen boarded the famous silver and blue train, from now on their moving residence across Canada. From the Quebec station for miles, spectators lined the right of way and at every station groups of country people were waiting to catch a glimpse of the Royal train.

Another royal visit in 1964 was greeted with rather less fervid acclaim, as journalist Blair Fraser reported:

The Queen arrived the next morning. Instead of going in to watch her inspect the guard of honour (a ritual which took place inside the big freight and customs shed, thus screened from public view), I stood outside by the steel fence behind which about four hundred people had gathered to greet her. They raised a rather squeaky cheer as she came down the gangplank – not very loud, but almost as loud as the one in Charlottetown four days before ...

The RCMP's instructions were to pay no attention to placard-carriers or demonstrators so long as they were orderly, to use force only to make arrests or in self-defence, and in no circumstances to inflict injury on anyone. Unfortunately the Quebec City police seemed to have had different instructions.

There were four major encounters between the city police and the crowd during the day, and every one took place in the absence of the Queen ... All that she saw or heard, if anything, was a crowd chanting slogans such as "Québec aux Québecois" and, on two or three brief occasions, shouting "boo" and "Élisabeth chez vous." A few young men turned their backs as the Queen's car went by. They were certainly very rude, and their parents must have felt ashamed of them, but they never offered or even threatened any violence.

It was after the Queen had passed (or, in one instance, at a place she never went near) that the Quebec City police charged into the crowd with clubs swinging. This was the only violence of the day ... Reporters saw, and in several cases photographed, dozens of ... assaults. Some were hit themselves, and painfully though not seriously hurt. The effect was one that we'd have thought impossible a few hours before – sympathy for the young demonstrators who, rude and ill-behaved though they were, had certainly not provoked this sort of treatment.

The royal visit of 1939, Château Frontenac.

"Not sorry our masters are leaving"

Language laws

Most of the resentment towards anglophones focused on language. The first law governing the use of French in Quebec was the Lavergne Law, passed in 1910, requiring that tickets for buses, trains and trams be printed in both French and English. In 1937, Duplessis passed a law requiring the French text of Quebec laws to prevail over the English, reasoning that the French would better reflect the intent of the lawmakers. It was repealed the following year.

When Jean-Jacques Bertrand's government introduced legislation in 1969 ratifying the idea that people could choose the language in which their children were to be educated, 30,000 people protested in front of the Parliament buildings against parents being given this option. That same year, the Gendron Commission held public hearings on the language issue. While Price Brothers pulp and paper company representatives were testifying at the CEGEP Sainte-Foy auditorium, students threw bottles and sticks at the commissioners, drowning out discussion with shouts of *"Lâches!"* (cowards) and *"Niaiseux!"* (idiots). The hearings had to be moved elsewhere. Alexandre Labrecque, vice-president of Price Brothers, said that while French was the dominant language of work at the company, English was the language of business. The company required English to be spoken by its engineers, accountants, administrators, economists, lawyers, salesmen, chemists, geologists and labour advisors.

In 1973, William Tetley, minister of financial institutions in Robert Bourassa's government, rewrote the Companies Act so that Quebec businesses were now required to adopt a French name, with the option of having an English or bilingual name too. Of the 60,000 companies notified, fewer than 25 complied. Then Tetley personally wrote to 500 presidents of top companies. Only a handful volunteered to comply, the others offering as their reason, "It is not in our interests."

In the face of this intransigence, Bourassa's Liberals introduced the first major law restricting the use of English in 1974. Bill 22 legislated French as Quebec's only official language, and resulted in immigrant children being tested on their English before being allowed to go to English schools. Education Minister François Cloutier said, "Any increases in the English school system will be based on children whose maternal language is English. The English system will not grow from francophone parents sending their children to English schools, [nor] by using the influx of immigrants who are not anglophone."

Manhattan Café, Rue Saint-Jean, ca. 1935.
In 1933 the Association Catholique de la Jeunesse Canadienne-française counted up the signs along two of Quebec's main streets, and found that of 499 signs, 243 were in French, 125 were bilingual and 131 were in English only. Many of the English signs were advertising businesses run by Chinese, Jewish or Greek immigrants. The Manhattan Café, owned by Greek immigrant Dan Shilakos, opened on Côte du Palais in the 1920s and later moved to Rue Saint-Jean. The family had its own linguistic priorities: it opened a school in 1930 that taught Greek to the children of Greek immigrants.

Although Bill 22 contained many provisions for the protection of the anglophones of Quebec, the revolt of English speakers against the bill was virulent in some parts of Montreal. In Quebec City protest was muted, not least because by the 1970s the only anglophones in the provincial legislature were from Montreal and did not always reflect the opinions of Quebec City anglophones. Established anglophone families were not worried: many had been bilingual for generations, and some were now sending their children to French schools. But immigrants whose first language was neither French nor English were upset, and people of every language shared their dismay at the idea of subjecting tiny children to formal exams. Quebec City's Chinese families took the bull by the horns and sent their toddlers to English lessons over the summer of 1974 to qualify them for English kindergarten. Francophones who wanted to ensure that their children were bilingual by sending them to English schools rushed to register their children before the portcullis came down. Some francophones were content with the legislation, while others didn't think it went nearly far enough.

Some Quebec anglophone intellectuals tried to understand the new nationalism and communicate it to their fellow English-speakers, such as Quebec City poet F.R. Scott, who translated a book of political essays called *Quebec States its Case*. Another source of support was an increasing number of American draft dodgers arriving in Quebec to avoid being sent to Vietnam. They were better able to accept the new minority status being accorded to anglophones than many of the old guard, and had integrated well into both cultures by enrolling at Laval University and various language schools in the city. As a group who felt similarly oppressed by their respective rulers, they supported the nationalists, as did other anglophones who saw the movement as akin to the struggles against colonial oppression going on in Vietnam, Ireland and many parts of Africa.

The majority hung tight to see what would happen, but many spoke with their actions: in the 1960s English speakers were two and half times more likely to leave Quebec than French speakers, and between 1971 and 1986, 198,274 English speakers left the province.

Anglophones who left Quebec were unmourned by the Parti Québécois government. Premier Lévesque said the two communities were "like scorpions in a bottle," and one of his cabinet ministers, Bernard Landry, declared himself "not sorry that our masters are leaving." For French speakers of Quebec, "les Anglais" represented a homogenous group with a distinct personality. But for the "Anglais" themselves, there was no collective identity to speak of. In Quebec City there were those of Irish, English, Scottish, Welsh, Italian, Jewish, eastern European, German, Chinese, Lebanese, Greek and American ancestry, all of whom were English speakers

Bill 22, 1974.

The profound cultural duality of Canada's origins was finally officially recognized by Ottawa in the much diluted forms of Canada-wide bilingualism and multiculturalism. Bilingualism may be a source of individual power, and may have helped stem the tide of assimilation for francophones in the west, but for francophone Quebecers it missed the point. Few Quebecers were happy with Bill 22, which proclaimed French as Quebec's official language but did not resolve the language issue to the satisfaction of either francophones or anglophones. Many anglophones left the Liberal Party in protest.

but who, until now, had little else in common other than that most wished to remain Canadians as well as Quebecers. Those who identified more with Canada than with Quebec were worried, as was Pierre Elliott Trudeau. "I had a real sense that the country wouldn't last," he wrote. "It would become a confederation of shopping centres."

Those who didn't leave had to ask themselves some serious questions about their identity. French Canadians in Quebec now called themselves Québécois. Were anglophones still English Canadians, were they English Quebecers, or were they now Québécois too?

Love consists in this, that two solitudes protect and touch
and greet each other.

Rainer Maria Rilke

Since 1976

Language and nation

After 1976 the English speakers of Quebec City went through a sea change: perhaps the falling and then rising of a small tide. At first, economic ups and downs as well as new language legislation and a separatist movement led to an exodus of Quebec City anglophones, and those who remained were at a loss as to what their future would be in the city. Churches, schools and other institutions closed; others amalgamated. But then the tide turned. If numbers remained small, the surviving institutions and the new coalitions learned better how to live and indeed thrive together. Siege thinking was replaced by an intentional reaching out to anglophone newcomers and to the francophone majority. The new "knowledge-based" economy gave the English language a new place in the city. Anglophones began to take a new pride in their ethnic origins, their particular history in Quebec City, their bilingualism and their participation in the majority French-speaking society.

Chapter 5
The Anglos of Today

Being an English speaker in Quebec City in 2005 feels like living in a small village, where everyone knows someone who knows your father, gossip travels fast, and there's always somebody either to help you out or to stab you in the back. But the parochialism is only one part of English speakers' reality. They may be deeply involved in village affairs, but at the same time they are active citizens of a large cosmopolitan city. They can put on an amateur theatre production one night in the church hall in English, and the next night go to the opera at the Grand Théâtre in French. They can flip the dial from French to English Quebec City radio stations and feel equally at home with both. They can read *Le Soleil*, the *Quebec Chronicle-Telegraph* (Quebec City's English paper), *Le Devoir* or the *Montreal Gazette*. On Saturdays their children can play in a French soccer match in the morning and spend the afternoon in an English library.

L'Assemblée nationale, couleurs fauves,
Simon Carmichael, 2002.

Simon Carmichael was born in Quebec in 1953. The Carmichaels immigrated from County Antrim, Northern Ireland, in the 19th century. Like many Irish Catholic families, they quickly assimilated into the francophone community. His grandfather opened a haberdashery shop on Rue Saint-Joseph in 1915 and later moved it to Rue Saint-Jean, where it stood for more than 75 years. "I like painting landscape," says the artist. "It provides a basic structure to which I keep subtracting, rather than adding, until the painting finds its own balance and order." His work can be seen in galleries in Quebec, Montreal and Toronto.

My Fair Lady, Quebec Art Company, 2003.
Bilingual Quebecers can go to the theatre
in the language of their choice. The oldest
English theatre company in the city is the
Quebec Art Company. The Company began
its days as the Quebec Art Theatre in the 1940s,
putting on plays in the ballroom of the Château
Frontenac and the Institut Canadien. Its home
in the 1950s was an upper room in the Louis
Jolliet House on Little Champlain Street,
from where Harold Braff ran the Funiculaire and
the Quebec-Lévis ferry. The theatre company
closed down after 20 years of productions,
and reopened in 1980 under former member
Rosemary Cannon as the Quebec Art Company.

Marriage and memory

A *variegated village*

The English-speaking "village" in Quebec City is not a homoge-
neous group and does not reside in a single neighbourhood. Once
there were anglophone enclaves in the Quartier Champlain,
Montcalm and Sillery, but now they are to be found in every
corner of the city, and in every profession. There are university
professors, lawyers and accountants; there are house cleaners,
factory workers, carpenters, teachers and social workers; there are
soldiers and businesswomen, scientists and musicians. Some have
been here for generations, and others arrived a few weeks ago.
Some came here for a job or for a summer, and stayed because they
traversed the two solitudes and fell in love with a francophone – a
survey in 2000 revealed that about 43% of Quebec City's anglophones have francophone partners. Should we be surprised? As we
have seen, intermarriage is a tradition that dates back hundreds of
years: the Porters, Harveys, Sullivans and Daltons in Quebec City
today, all francophones, attest to a *métissage* that has been going on
since the eighteenth century.

Because of the historical assembling of all who were neither
Catholic nor French-speaking (such as Jews, Greeks and Chinese)
in the few English schools, English speakers are ethnically a very
mixed bunch too. Brian Treggett, who buries Quebecers at the
Mount Hermon Cemetery, calls it the "immigrants' graveyard."
The names on the headstones, dating back to 1848, originate in
almost every country in the world. Most of these families, once
they arrived in Quebec City, became English-speaking.

But English speakers of all origins are not only to be found in the
graveyard. There are about 9,000 in the "village" today (including
outlying communities in the Quebec Capitale Nationale region),
and they include people of Jewish, Chinese, American, German,
Ukrainian, Hungarian, Polish, Italian, Greek, Welsh, Armenian,
Russian, Kazakh, Indian and Lebanese origin. Many of those who
originated outside Britain or Ireland are trilingual, such as Anglo-
Quebecer Napoleon Woo, who switches easily between three
languages with his clients at the Wok n' Roll, his restaurant on
Boulevard Charest. Ninety per cent of English speakers in the
region know French, and the mother tongue of 6.7% of them is
neither English nor French. Over one quarter of anglophones living
in Quebec City in 2001 had moved here from elsewhere – nearly
half from the United States – within the past five years.

The way the members of the English-speaking communities talk to one another is unique to Quebec City, and probably nearly as old as the city itself. Young people switch from English to French in mid-sentence, depending on what they are talking about or who joins the conversation. Those at English schools, where a majority of the students are from French-speaking backgrounds, switch to French as soon as they walk out the schoolroom door. Distinct dialects and vocabularies have evolved within these communities, such as the English words incorporated into Greek spoken in Quebec City, and the French words incorporated into the English spoken here (see p. 119). Irish Quebecers have their own jokes that no one outside that particular community would understand.

In terms of money as well as ethnicity, these "Anglais" are now further than ever from the old stereotype of the rich anglo bosses. As in much of the Western world, the gap between the rich and the poor English speakers of Quebec City is widening. While one group is professional, well-educated and secure in their jobs, the other lacks education, job prospects and mobility. Fourteen per cent live below the poverty line.

This has perhaps always been the case, as the memories of today's anglos testify. Greek Orthodox Quebecers reminiscing in the basement of their church on Boulevard René-Lévesque recall holding their early religious meetings in garages and sheds. Jewish and Syrian Anglo-Quebecers recall their parents peddling with a backpack from door to door. Napoleon Woo recalls being deposited at the Roman Catholic St. Brigid's orphanage when he was six. Pavel de Liamchin, son of Russian immigrants, recalls his years in the Anglican Finlay Home on Sainte-Foy Road, which marked him for life, both for better and for worse.

Anglophones are invisibly present in the city's commercial and music communities, too. There are hotels, restaurants and pubs run by anglophones, and some of the calèches are the property of Russell Doyle, who owns the largest calèche company in the city. Equally important in the city's transportation economy are Paul Boardman (Cap Rouge) and Jay Manek (St. Roch), who sell skateboards. A quarter of the players in the Orchestre Symphonique de Québec are anglophones, and some of the city's most popular singers, such as Bob Walsh, Dorothée Berryman and Tess LeBlanc, are bilingual and bicultural.

Many francophones in the city do not even know that the anglophone community exists, partly because most English speakers are bilingual and well integrated into the francophone population, and partly because there are few signs, literally, of their presence. Anglophone newcomers, too, can live for years in Quebec City before discovering the presence of an English-speaking community.

Wok 'n' Roll Restaurant, Boulevard Charest.

Like many of Quebec City's earliest Chinese immigrants, the Woo and Wong families, still running restaurants and stores in the city, became anglophones. The Chinese first worked in hand laundries, and then moved into the restaurant business. But medium-budget family-run restaurants depend on young family members being willing to work long hours for little pay. Young Chinese are now moving into computers and other high tech industries, while some of the Chinese who have worked in Quebec restaurants all their lives are planning to retire back to China.

**Brian Treggett with historic notice board,
Mount Hermon Cemetery, 1999.**

This 100-year-old sign instructs visitors
to Mount Hermon Cemetery not to eat or drink
on the premises, drive their carriages at faster
than walking pace, hold parties or set their horses
loose in the graveyard. Trespassers are threatened
with imprisonment. In 1999 Brian Treggett,
whose ancestors have tended the cemetery since
1865, framed this notice board and covered it
with plexiglass. Quebec's Protestant anglophones
are increasingly proud of their "immigrant
cemetery," dating from 1845. Many non-
anglophones and non-Protestants are buried here
too, and today it is the cemetery of choice
for Quebec's Cambodian Buddhists.

Greek Orthodox Church of the Annunciation, 17 Boulevard René-Lévesque.

In 1915 Greek immigrants began to hold Greek Orthodox services in garages
and basements, and borrowed St. Matthew's Anglican Church for baptisms and
marriages. They hired John Konstantinides to teach their children Greek,
and acquired a lot in Mount Hermon Cemetery, still the cemetery for Orthodox
Quebecers to this day. The Orthodox parish of the Annunciation was
worshipping in the Institut Canadien in 1959 when it bought this large house
and converted it into a church. It is now the spiritual home of the Orthodox
Greeks, Russians and Serbians in town.

The long tongue of the law

Words and school

There were two shocks for the English-speaking communities of Quebec City in the last quarter of the twentieth century. The first occurred when the Parti Québécois, a party dedicated to separating Quebec from Canada, came to power in 1976. The second occurred in 1995, when a referendum to decide the question of sovereignty was won by the No side with a margin of only 1.2%.

One of the first things the Parti Québécois did when it came to power was to introduce the Charter of the French Language, or Bill 101, Quebec's most famous piece of language legislation. Facing one of the lowest birthrates in the world and afraid that the French language was drowning in a North American sea of English, Quebec obliged all immigrants to attend French schools. The English speakers of Quebec City found themselves defined as never before: no one who immigrated to Quebec after 1977 could educate their children in English, unless one parent had attended an English elementary school in Quebec. All communication in the public domain was to be in French, including signs. People set to work across the city to eliminate any visible vestiges of an English presence.

Quebec's Protestant school boards, for one, were relieved. At last the confusions and ambiguities of the Liberals' attempt to deal with the language issue, Bill 22, were cleared up. One newly formed anglophone organization, however, was less than enchanted.

A few months before the Charter became law, a group calling itself the Metropolitan Quebec Language Rights Committee called a public meeting at the Château Frontenac. Twelve hundred anglophones sang "O Canada" before ratifying a brief entitled "To Be or Not to Be," in which the committee strongly opposed the proposed legislation. The brief objected particularly to the preamble to Bill 1, the original version of Bill 101, which proclaimed that "the French language has always been the language of the Quebec people."

"Do you remember the good old days of Bill 22?"
Raoul Hunter, *Le Soleil*, April 27, 1977.

Bill 22, under which immigrant children had to take an entrance test to qualify for English schools, not only upset some anglophones; it also displeased francophones because aside from the tests there was still freedom of choice in language of education. When Bill 101 came along three years later, it pushed the matter home by restricting English education to those with a parent who had attended school in English in Quebec. This rule affected new immigrants, but also those Quebec anglophones who had been sent to French schools to learn the language, and were now prevented from sending their own children to English schools.

97

"One can only conclude," stated the brief, "that those residents whose language is not French are not part of the Quebec people." It attributed any bad feeling between English- and French-speaking Quebecers to "an ugly religious barrier erected by ancestors who brought this virus with them from a Europe plagued with religious intolerance," but noted that there were always "sufficient people of good will on both sides of the religious barrier who managed to rescue us from the destructive climate of religious intolerance." Writers Gary Ouellet and Dominic Macdonald feared that the enshrinement of linguistic intolerance would now relegate the community to the history books. "We oppose [Cultural Development Minister Camille] Laurin's proposal," they wrote, "for the very same reason his ancestors opposed Lord Durham's solution [assimilation of French Canadians]." The offending preamble was altered for Bill 101, but little else was.

Enrolment in English schools in Montreal plummeted, but in Quebec City there was little impact on numbers. While many anglophones no longer qualified for certificates of eligibility for English schooling, more francophones who did qualify enrolled their children in the English school system. The language of the schoolyard was thus increasingly French. Marianna O'Gallagher, a former teacher at St. Patrick's High School, illustrated the situation:

The English kids in English schools didn't feel like teaching the other kids to speak English, so they just spoke to them in French. One teacher told me he was monitoring a grade 8 exam and he put the exam papers down on the table and said, "You kids sit still, and when I give the signal you can turn over the page and start." Immediately half the kids turned to the other half and said, "Qu'est-ce qu'il dit?" [What's he saying?].

But English-speaking communities could no longer grow except by having lots more babies, attracting Canadians from other provinces or integrating allophone immigrants who spoke both English and French in addition to their mother tongue. Fewer English speakers arrived to replace those who left, and immigration policies favouring French-speaking peoples meant that the percentage of immigrants whose mother tongue was English dropped from nearly 20% in 1975 to less than 3% in 1996.

At the same time, some English speakers felt invisible and excluded. Street names that had reflected the presence of anglophones in the city had mostly disappeared, and all other outward signs of their presence were literally forbidden. A special language police, known to anglophones as "the tongue troopers," ferreted out infringements of the sign law. They paid a visit to the principal of St. Patrick's High School to tell him that the sign above the door reading *St. Patrick's High School* had to be changed, because it was in English. When they argued that "French is our *patrimoine*," the principal replied, "We have a *patrimoine* too," and sent them packing.

Graven in stone: Signs of Quebec City's anglophone history still visible today.

Bill 101, enacted in 1977, declared that French was the official language of Quebec and that public signs, posters and public advertising were henceforth to be solely in French, with exceptions in certain circumstances. Political commentator Josée Legault called the law "shock therapy": signs of an anglophone presence in Quebec were literally wiped out. But attentive observers can still find visible traces in Quebec City in the form of painted advertisements high on the walls of old industrial buildings, or signs that remain only because they were engraved in stone.

28227

DÉCLARATION D'ADMISSIBILITÉ
A L'ENSEIGNEMENT EN ANGLAIS

La personne soussignée déclare que

Timothy   **Stavert**   **STAT 000000 00**

né le **1990-12-31**, peut recevoir l'enseignement en anglais en vertu de **l'article 73 paragraphe 1** de la Charte de la langue française.

2005-02-17
Date de la décision

Personne désignée par le ministre

This certificate of eligibility does not prevent a child from receiving instruction in French. In that case, the child will be "deemed to have received or be receiving instruction in English" within the meaning of section 76.1 of the *Charter of the French language.*

Certificate of eligibility.

Since 1977, Quebec pupils have been required to present a certificate of eligibility such as this one to qualify for English schooling. Although some anglophones were peeved, Andrew Roy, then Director General of the Eastern Quebec Regional School Board, recalled, "It was a relief to work with a policy that could be applied at the school level with a minimum of confusion." New immigrants to Quebec now had to send their children to French schools, while Quebec's older immigrant population, such as the Jarjours, an Orthodox Syrian family that arrived in Quebec in the 1920s, continued for the most part to educate their children in English.

Holding up the roof

Jobs and English institutions

English speakers still had no place in the civil service, and the recession of the 1980s propelled a general exodus in search of jobs. The tables had well and truly turned in 20 years, and now young people with English names were less likely to get jobs in Quebec. As McGill University Chancellor Gretta Chambers said (in French), "When you hire someone, you naturally choose someone you know, someone you can talk to easily, someone who will laugh at your jokes. You even find such a person more intelligent!"

Even for outsiders operating in Quebec, hiring francophones was more politically correct. Some francophones interpreted the exodus of large numbers of English speakers as a sign that Anglo-Quebecers were simply not attached to Quebec, but the vast majority of Anglo-Quebecers were bilingual, and as such were mobile and in demand elsewhere in Canada. Many ex-Quebecers still make annual pilgrimages back to Quebec City and think of themselves strongly and fondly as Quebecers.

The English speakers who remained tended to be the ones who understood the aspirations of francophones, who had francophone partners or were connected to them through friendships and work, and who were determined to weather difficult times. But the population base for the institutions that had served them had dropped drastically.

The *Quebec Chronicle-Telegraph*, which claims to be the oldest continuously published newspaper in North America, was reduced from a daily with prestigious offices on Buade Street to a weekly community newspaper operated on a shoestring out of the publisher's own basement. Subscriptions dropped to about a thousand, and even after René Lévesque took out a subscription in 1982, there was no mass adhesion among French-speakers. Another group that found itself in a basement was the CBC, which opened a radio station in 1979 to serve the whole of English-speaking Quebec outside Montreal, including the Magdalen Islands, the Gaspé, the Eastern Townships and the North Shore as well as Quebec City.

D-Day veteran Mervin Jones, 80 years old, surrounded by modern day paratroopers of the Battalion Royal Regiment, Valcartier, 2003.

A jewel in the crown of the city's military heritage is Mervin Jones, the only airborne D-Day vet living in the Quebec City region. At 1 a.m. on June 6, 1944, just before the massive Allied beach landings, he parachuted into Normandy with the 1st Canadian Parachute Battalion with a mandate to blow up bridges and knock out German command centres. Only half of the unit lived to tell the tale. Mervin Jones was scoutmaster for 47 years and lives in Valcartier.

St. Matthew's Anglican Church, now the Bibliothèque Saint-Jean-Baptiste.

St. Peter's Anglican Church, Limoilou, under demolition.

English churches had seen a big drop in attendance even before the exodus, similar to the decline in French churches. Yet most of the buildings remained. Some of these were turned over to the francophone community. The Methodist church on Rue Sainte-Angèle and St. Matthew's Anglican Church on Rue Saint-Jean are now French public libraries, St. Vincent's Church is a school board conference room, the Baptist church on Rue McMahon is a gay bathhouse and St. Patrick's Church on Rue McMahon is a cancer research centre for Hôtel-Dieu Hospital. The tiny congregations in the remaining churches spend most of their money and energy trying to prevent the buildings, most of them historic monuments, from tumbling down around their ears. In 2005 there were still ten functioning English-speaking churches in Quebec City, few with congregations of more than 30 or 40 people. The Beth Israel Ohev Sholom synagogue has had weekly visits from a Montreal rabbi since the 1950s, and the Greek Orthodox Church of the Annunciation makes do with a visiting priest on Sundays.

English-language welfare institutions, founded during the nineteenth century to care for needy anglophone immigrants, were taken over by the state or closed. The Ladies' Protestant Home on Grande Allée, a final home for many of Quebec's anglophone servants, closed in 1989 and was converted into condominiums, while St. Brigid's Home, formerly a Roman Catholic orphanage, became the old-age home for all English speakers. The Jeffery Hale Hospital, founded for "Protestants of all denominations" lost its status as the only English hospital serving eastern Quebec and was converted into a long-term care facility, although it managed to keep emergency services and an outpatient clinic. English-speaking doctors were retiring or leaving. There were no more front-line medical services for English speakers in their own language.

Some of the changes were for the better: the Garrison Club, by force of circumstance, lost some of its exclusive reputation and accepted Jews and women as members for the first time. The University Women's Club, still raising money for study bursaries for English-speaking women, struck the word "University" from its name, reduced its membership fee and began to accept full membership from non-university-educated women. This breaking down of barriers heralded a change of heart in the community.

Quebec Chronicle-Telegraph team:
Mike Reshitnyk, Matthew Anderson,
Marcella Smit, Karen Macdonald, François
Vézina and Michèle Thibeau, 1999.

In 1979 the *Quebec Chronicle-Telegraph*, North America's oldest surviving newspaper, looked as though its chips were up. Four Quebecers, David Cannon, Jean Lemelin, Ross Rourke and Bob Dawson, saved it from an ignominious end, and a few years later David Cannon acquired sole ownership. In 1993 it was bought by Karen Macdonald and François Vézina. The *Chronicle-Telegraph*, now more than 240 years old, is published every Wednesday out of the owners' basement in Sainte-Foy. Its circulation in 2005 was 1,800.

Auction at closing of Ladies' Protestant Home, July 7, 1990.

With the sudden closing of the Home and the removal of its 39 residents, another anglophone institution met its demise and its contents – furniture, linen and dishes that had been accumulating there since its founding in 1859 – were auctioned to the four winds. The nursing staff found other jobs before the last residents had left, and volunteer Barbara Bignell had to take care of them herself, sleeping there and inviting friends to lunch to keep the residents company at mealtimes.

Living Witness

Lupita Kerwin was one of five young people who started a CBC radio station in 1979. Only one of the team, Dennis Trudeau, had any radio experience, and the executive producer, Doug Carr, was a philosophy graduate. Their initiation was abrupt.

"Quebec City was the only capital in Canada that did not have a CBC English station. It made no sense not to have a national broadcaster here, especially in those days when the constitution and confederation were being looked at afresh. In the spring of 1979 we started the morning show in Quebec City. At first no one was happy: Quebec City didn't want to hear about weather in the Gaspé, and the regions were upset because they didn't hear when someone they knew died.

"We started broadcasting in the sub-basement of the Auberge des Gouverneurs, where the station was still under construction. We had to go to the restaurant for our story meetings to hear ourselves speak.

"We were called to the front lines almost immediately, as the referendum was set for May 1980. In the six weeks leading up to May 20, we did a one-hour live insert that was heard on all the morning shows across the province. Each Monday we talked to a Liberal and a Péquiste minister, the next day to the political analysts, then to ordinary people. We were always running over to the National Assembly, and those 'terrifying' Péquistes became our best friends. They wanted to win this referendum, but didn't want to make an enemy of the other side, so they loved the chance to explain themselves to the rest of the country through us. The French journalists envied the privileged access we had.

"It wasn't like an election: something fundamental was at stake. It wasn't about a change of regime but a fundamental change in the future of a people. Knowing the people who were bringing this about, first hand, made things understandable, justifiable, approachable, but it didn't take away from the fear all around you. People in the English community were living in uncertainty and terrible fear.

"But when the No side won [59.5% to 40.5%], and René Lévesque said, 'À la prochaine fois' ['until next time'], it wasn't angry or bitter. It was okay; the ugliness subsided. People reacted with relief or resignation, nothing violent. But for us journalists, it was quite a hangover. Overnight we had to switch from covering the disappearance of the country to covering new traffic rules."

Lupita Kerwin

Dennis Trudeau and Lupita Kerwin.

Referendum signs outside Mount Hermon Cemetery, 1980.

Pride goes before a FOLS

The anglo identity crisis

There was a still a lot of soul-searching among those who remained in Quebec City. What is it that distinguished Anglo-Quebecers from Anglo-Canadians? Who is a Québécois? Can one go out on Saint-Jean-Baptiste Day and wave a fleur-de-lis and talk English? Can one go out on Canada Day and wave a maple leaf and still be considered a good Québécois? Can one do both?

Anglophones were ill-at-ease. "People were afraid to speak English in public; we were wary of our actions," said Lupita Kerwin. "I had friends who stopped speaking to me during the referendum because I was an anglophone, people I'd known all my life. It was the closest it ever came to feeling like Ireland. I hated it: something unnatural had taken hold of us."

Publisher and broadcaster Karen Macdonald remembered, "As kids, we didn't speak English in public very much. If we were on the bus, we just wouldn't talk, or we would talk French. I don't remember people saying nasty things to me: we just presumed that people didn't really like you if you were English, and so we didn't want to take any chances."

If this wasn't enough of an identity crisis, there were other questions. Is there one English-speaking community in Quebec City, or several? Is an anglophone an Anglo-Quebecer *de souche*, that is, someone who, up to 1977 (Bill 101), had joined a historic culture that dates back 200 years and more? Or a "FOLS" (First Official Language Spoken): someone who speaks English but not necessarily as their mother tongue? Or again, is it someone who chooses to speak English as their day-to-day language of communication? Depending on their history, politics and aims, on the person who asks them, and even on the moment when the question is asked, Quebec City's English speakers plump for one of many possible identities.

Anglophone Quebecers found identity issues confusing even outside Quebec. Andrew Roy, Director of the Eastern Quebec Regional School Board, was invited to Saskatchewan in 1981 by the Association Culturelle Franco-Canadienne. When he suggested on a radio call-in show that French school boards be established and controlled by Fransaskois, all callers were violently opposed to any special privileges for French speakers, and roundly chewed him out for suggesting it. "As someone who as a boy had seldom known what it was to have 25 cents in his pocket, it was difficult to see myself as my listeners probably did: a fat cat from the east representing the Liberal government."

With no more representation in Parliament, and numbers already low and plummeting, Anglo-Quebecers were finally forced to contemplate themselves as a silent minority instead of historical cocreators of Quebec society. Both of Quebec's major political parties, the Liberals and the Parti Québécois, were more concerned with empowering the francophone majority than with protecting the English-speaking minorities, and in federal politics, the party in power struggled to keep francophone Quebecers within the country. In this less than promising political landscape, Anglo-Quebecers began to form special-interest lobbying groups.

Alliance Quebec was formed in Montreal as an interest group to fight for the rights of English-speaking Quebecers. In 1981 Voice of English Quebec (VEQ), an outgrowth of the group that four years earlier had called a meeting at the Château Frontenac to protest the Parti Québécois' language legislation, was formed to speak for English speakers in Quebec City. Quebec City anglophones didn't always see things the way English-speaking Montrealers did. They were more likely to be bilingual, more integrated into the French-speaking majority and more likely to understand the collective aspirations of French speakers. In the constitutional debates of the 1980s, VEQ distinguished itself from Montreal-based Alliance Quebec by opposing the patriation of the constitution by the federal government without Quebec's approval (until then, Canada's constitution was an act of the British Parliament). VEQ supported both the Meech Lake Accord and the Charlottetown Agreement, which would have recognized Quebec as a distinct society within Canada. Neither agreement was ratified by all provinces.

Living Witness

Patrick Donovan was born in Quebec City in 1975. He went to elementary school in English, high school in French, CEGEP in English, studied for his BA in English at Concordia in Montreal and for his MA in French at l'Université de Montréal. He is now conservation and interpretation advisor at the Morrin Centre.

"Like many teenagers in high school, I was socially awkward and my peers took delight in pestering me, though the nature of the taunting changed when I transferred from English to French school. All of a sudden, I had become a British imperialist seeking to subjugate the French, or I was held responsible for all the Yanqui smut seeping into the country from the south. Outright nonsense, in part because my ancestors had been poor French, Slovak and Irish farmers, but moreso because it is absurd to be held accountable for things you have nothing to do with just because your first language is English. I laugh now when I remember being told to 'go back to Ontario' even though I had never set foot in the province. The need to fit in is important during adolescence, so I became the most militant Quebec separatist imaginable for a few years, waving *patriote* flags at rallies and such. Eventually, I settled into non-ideological adulthood. Nowadays I'm more interested in supporting whatever political party promotes sustainable development and heritage conservation, whether separatist or federalist, than in language or the national question."

Patrick Donovan

Saint-Jean-Baptiste Day.

In the 1970s and early 1980s, some anglophones felt afraid to speak English in public, and wondered if they were welcome to celebrate Saint-Jean-Baptiste Day along with francophone Quebecers. During the period of the referendum, friendships were ruptured and families divided. "Something unnatural had taken hold of us," said broadcaster Lupita Kerwin.

After a Supreme Court challenge to a law requiring that all commercial signs be in French, Bill 178 (1988) was a compromise that permitted bilingual signs *inside* commercial establishments. As the sign laws still violated both the Quebec Charter of Human Rights and Freedoms and the Canadian Charter of Rights and Freedoms, the Liberal government used the controversial exemptions in those charters known as the "notwithstanding" clauses. Three anglophone cabinet ministers resigned in protest.

Again, Saskatchewan invited anglophone Quebec to visit, and again, Quebec City refused to play victim. This time VEQ past president David Blair was the guest. "Seeing how francophones are treated in Saskatchewan helps one put into perspective the importance of Bill 178," he said. Some Montreal politicians were "spreading the word around Canada that Anglo-Quebecers in the province of Quebec are an oppressed minority," he added. "It isn't true."

Over the years English speakers succeeded in winning the right to post bilingual signs outside too, as long as French was dominant. They won the right to an English education for English speakers with a parent who had been educated in English in *Canada*, and not just Quebec, in 1982, and guarantees of education and social services in English in 1986.

Meech Lake.

With Quebec's signature still missing from the 1982 Canadian constitution, the Meech Lake Accord (1987) was an attempt to give constitutional recognition to Quebec's distinctiveness. It was hammered out in a marathon meeting in a lakeside lodge by Prime Minister Brian Mulroney and the ten provincial premiers, including Quebec premier Robert Bourassa. However, two provinces, Newfoundland and Manitoba, failed to ratify it before the three-year deadline. Voice of English Quebec, representing the region's minority anglophones, backed the accord.

Coming alive again

New anglophone organizations

Gradually the "English-speaking community" *became* a community, with a cultural identity that was perhaps partly formed (some would say invented) by the new experience of being a minority. "Up to 30 or 40 years ago," said Karen Macdonald, "Catholics and Protestants didn't talk to each other and old-stock anglophones didn't socialize with newcomers. But because of shrinking numbers, assimilation and the loss of institutions, people felt the need to come closer together and build a community." Taking the assets that remained of the old institutions, the community built them into new foundations and institutions that served all English speakers. The largest of these is the Holland Centre.

With resources from the now-closed Ladies' Protestant Home and six other "old" institutions, the Holland Centre opened with a staff of four in 1991 to offer services to old people. It hired a demographer to count who was left in the English-speaking community, and asked them what they needed. Soon it expanded its services to all age groups, and began travelling around to scattered anglophones in outlying villages to provide the services *in situ*. In 1997, it entered into partnerships with the local CLSC (community health centre), St. Brigid's Home, the Jeffery Hale Hospital and the Centre Jeunesse de Québec (youth protection agency). In less than ten years the English community went from having no front-line services devoted to the English-speaking population to having a full range. The Holland Centre now has a total budget of more than $1.6 million and a staff of 30.

"At first the CLSCs were uncomfortable with sharing their resources and didn't understand the Holland Centre's viewpoint," said Diane Kameen, information agent at the centre. "Now they are more accepting. The Holland Centre still has to be careful. It can't call itself an English CLSC, for example."

Some English-speaking institutions have moved from a siege role to a proactive role. The Holland Centre has gained an international reputation with its homegrown method of providing community-based services for a minority. St. Brigid's Home has opened a wing that is pioneering a new approach to caring for people suffering from Alzheimer's. The Literary and Historical Society, once reduced to auctioning off its treasures, has expanded into the Morrin Centre, a cultural centre that highlights anglophone contributions to Quebec City history. "It's no longer the garrisoned bastion of francophone anglophiles and old-stock anglophone Protestant culture," said Patrick Donovan, who works there. "The Lit and Hist is broadening its horizons." In 2004, for example, it celebrated Bloomsday, more popular in Ireland than St. Patrick's Day, and had an evening of Bollywood: "We have events in French about the English, and we also have lots of general cultural events that have nothing to do with interpreting Anglo community history. The strength of the English-speaking population in Quebec City is that it is integrated. We are going to build on that strength."

Indeed there are many integrated anglophones in Quebec City who have no affiliation with the anglophone institutions at all, and deliberately distance themselves for fear of being trapped in a claustrophobic Anglo ghetto. Peter Vaughan comes from Toronto but has lived in Quebec City for 30 years. He runs the city's last remaining English-language bookstore. "I've never identified with the anglophone gang," he said. "I didn't really see the need. I'm an Anglo in a Québécois environment, and I like that." He calls VEQ "a support group that would perish without federal funding," and believes that, except for the Holland Centre, the Anglo community should survive without government support: "If they want to live, they will live!"

When it comes time to sending children to school, however, the identity issue comes more sharply into focus.

Morrin Centre.

The Morrin Centre is the fourth vocation of this building in the heart of the Old City. First of all a prison (1808–1867), then a Presbyterian college (1868–1904), this graceful building stood empty for 100 years except for the rooms occupied by the Literary and Historical Society Library. In keeping with a new acceptance of Anglos as having an important place in the city's history, in 2005 it received public funding for restoration into an interpretation centre for Quebec's anglophone heritage.

English immersion

The new reality of English schools

After the creation of a Ministry of Education in 1964 and a new system of public secondary schools, the state had gradually taken over the domain of education. From 1971–1972 school boards were amalgamated to form large boards out of the 1,100 smaller, local and autonomous ones that had existed earlier. The new Eastern Quebec Regional School Board was formed from 20 old ones, and set up shop in Bishop Mountain School, an old Anglican school in Sillery. Anglophone numbers in the Protestant school board were perilously low until a "white knight" appeared on the horizon in the form of growing numbers of Protestant francophones, who helped the Protestant board survive and thrive for a few more years.

In 1998, the historic denominational school boards that had been dividing children since the early nineteenth century into Catholics and Protestants, whatever their language, were abolished, and children were henceforth divided according to language instead. Irish Catholic Quebecers were in the same schools as Protestants for the first time, and French-speaking Protestants were among children whose families were, nominally at least, Catholic.

The new linguistic boards helped to break down some of the old divides that still separated the English-speaking communities. Aline Visser was nominated chair of the transitional board in 1998. With a Greek Orthodox mother and a Lebanese Catholic father, she described herself as a "*pure laine* Lebanese Québécoise," and was chosen as a neutral party acceptable to both Catholics and Protestants. "The law forced an issue that was long overdue," she said. "Linguistic boards are absolutely to the advantage of the English-speaking community. We are not as *borné* [blinkered] as we used to be, and the anglophone Protestants no longer see things in terms of 'us and them.' There's a new Québécois being invented, a new English-speaking community."

Four English schools in Quebec City (horizontally from top left): Holland Elementary School, St. Partick's High School, St. Vincent's School and Quebec High School.

The majority of students in Quebec's English schools are francophones. Students often switch languages in midsentence, or speak a mixture of both. While they may be orally and technologically bilingual, text-messaging in English isn't the same as to being able to read and write about *Hamlet* or even *Catcher in the Rye*. Educators have questions: Are students learning to write both languages well enough? If the schools accommodate francophones by adapting the curriculum, will the quality of education for anglophones suffer? If they don't, will the schools lose the numbers they need to remain open? And more immediately: in what language does one address the students on graduation day?

English-speaking educational institutions in the Quebec City region include one CEGEP, three high schools, six elementary schools and a vocational centre. Quebec City's English schools are perhaps the most vibrant of the community institutions. They employ large numbers of English speakers, and provide a social nucleus for students who must often travel long distances from far-flung areas of the region. "The schools have something special," said Patrick McKenna. "It's not just the language – it's also the community life. A lot of our kids are bused in from a great distances. Some of them arrive at 6 am and leave at 9 pm, after basketball practice or whatever. It's like a community centre."

But the schools are nevertheless fragile. In many families, two English-speaking parents send their children to French schools. With 70% of the students coming from francophone or bilingual homes (with parents assimilated into francophone culture), and 50% arriving at school with no English at all, they are becoming English immersion schools.

"If the schools water down the Englishness of their curriculum to accommodate the francophones, then do the anglophones suffer owing to the lower quality of English?" asked Bruce Willett, a former high school principal and a fifth-generation Quebecer. "The youth tend to be technologically literate, but can they read *Hamlet*? They can if they are the lucky ones who have been raised with books, conversation and respectful listening. Otherwise, if they have language difficulties, they are going to stay with [American rap singer] Eminem."

Especially in the schools, Quebec City's bilingual anglophones have developed their own dialect and specific language behaviours. The situation may be an educator's nightmare, but it's an anthropologist's dream. "We like to mix both languages, to start the sentence with one language and end it with another one," said Marc Drolet (St. Lawrence CEGEP). "Some things you can say better in French and some others better in English," said Rita Devlin, who doesn't know what box to tick when she is asked about her mother tongue. "In relationships, you usually stay in the language you start off in," said Eric Blair (Quebec High School). "When I say 'hi' to someone, whether they answer 'hello' or 'âllo' tells me what language they want to carry on in." "We usually switch to French as soon as we leave the classroom," said his sister Justine (Holland Elementary School), "unless we're in the middle of a conversation."

Trilingual Quebecers live with further complexities. "We speak Gujarati at home because my father's from India," said Prachi Shah (St. Lawrence CEGEP). "I also speak English with my parents occasionally, and with my sister I sometimes speak French when I don't want my parents to understand."

Living Witness

Prachi Shah is a second-generation Quebecer whose family is from India. She was educated in English schools in Quebec City.

"I wouldn't say I'm anglophone because it would be cutting out the French part. I wouldn't say I'm francophone either, and I wouldn't say I'm allophone. When I'm here I like to waive the whole minority immigrant thing. When I'm outside Quebec City I'm proud to be from here, and when I'm outside Quebec I say I'm Québécoise, and when I'm outside Canada, I'm proud to be Canadian!

"There are lots of people who speak English in Quebec who don't necessarily identify themselves with the anglophone organizations here. People who work in them are from certain families who have stayed here when they could have left, and there's a certain protective instinct. But they're definitely opening up their horizons. The community is changing, becoming more ethnic and diverse, with less of a cultural attachment to its English/Irish roots. When you're a minority, people stick together, but they also integrate, and English is something that can be kept. People just move on. The language isn't in danger, but some of the people are, since young people are leaving Quebec."

Prachi Shah

Economy needs English

A new role for the community

Tourism is an industry that has traditionally employed English speakers, as many visitors speak English. One of the top ten world tourist destinations, according to Condé Nast, Quebec City attracts nearly five million visitors every year, and tourism is responsible for 24,000 jobs.

Some of the anglophones who moved to Quebec City in the 1990s were responding to the city's changing economy. The new global economy had not been kind to either the anglophone-dominated older industries or the francophone-dominated government-based industries and public service sector (40% of Quebec jobs are in the federal, provincial or municipal government), and about 12,000 jobs were lost between 1993 and 2003. The increasing desire among francophone businesses and individuals to learn English provided jobs for many anglophones in second-language teaching, and the translation of documents into English provided other jobs. But there were also new job opportunities in high tech and biotechnology companies (or "knowledge-based industries"). As scientists presenting papers around the world usually do so in English, and English is also the language of international commerce and marketing, bilingual workers are in high demand, and many have been attracted to the city.

But for newcomers, uncovering the hidden face of the anglophone community in Quebec City can be a challenge. "Single anglophones have a hard time finding us," said Jennifer Alexander, a VEQ worker whose job is to link newcomers with Anglo institutions. "People with children are the first to find us, as they eventually get in touch with school boards and programs for kids." The moment when anglophones have children is also when many people start to think about the culture they are passing on to the next generation.

David Rompré conducting the Rhapsodes in the Easter Oratorio at Saint-Thomas-d'Aquin Church, July 2002.

The City of Quebec is renowned for its love of classical music, and many anglophone musicians have been attracted to the city to join the Opéra de Québec, Les Violons du Roi or the Orchestre Symphonique de Québec. Local anglophones participate enthusiastically in the dozens of other orchestras, ensembles and choirs in the city. David Rompré teaches music at Quebec High School, is director of the choir Les Rhapsodes and directs the choir of the Orchestre Symphonique de Québec.

Roots revival

Taking stock of the past

North American mobility and cultural rootlessness have sent many people in search of the stories of their ancestors. The Anglo-Quebec exodus and identity crisis of the 1970s and 1980s perhaps had the same effect. Many anglophones, not satisfied with being defined purely in terms of language, started to take a new interest in their ethnic roots and the distinctiveness of their culture. "Learning English words is not the same as having grown up in an English culture," said Quebec City historian Lorraine O'Donnell. "It's a much broader frame of reference: an intuitive sense of what is English, with the literature, the subtle humour, oral and written wordplay, and the fact that language is associated with a specific place that has its own culture, politics and social history."

Many of the mutual aid societies of Quebec City were based on country of origin, such as the St. Patrick's (Ireland), St. George's (England) and St. Andrew's (Scotland) societies. They have mostly died a quiet death, and are buried with their archives. But early in the twenty-first century new signs of life began to appear.

Irish Quebecers were the first to take serious stock of their past. In 2005 they were still the only anglophone group from Quebec City on whom any substantial research had been done. Among the people who formed the Irish Heritage Society were world-renowned atomic physicist Larkin Kerwin and Marianna O'Gallagher, historian of Irish Quebec City and publisher of Carraig Books, specializing in Irish Quebec City history. Both were later recognized with the Order of Canada.

Among the activities of Irish Heritage were the Irish Summer of 1997 and the development of Grosse Île National Historic Site and the Irish Memorial into a National Historic Site. Kerwin and O'Gallagher wanted the quarantine station at Grosse Île, where so many Irish had both begun and ended their lives in Canada, to become an important historical monument for those of Irish descent right across the country. They did not accomplish this without a struggle. As O'Gallagher tells the story,

> Parks Canada's marketing people didn't want to emphasize the deaths at Grosse Île. In their report they wrote, "The unfortunate events of the past, 1832 and 1847, will not be overemphasized." That was like waving a red flag in front of a bull as far as we were concerned. They didn't know the Irish. The Irishman's sports page is the obituaries! There was an outcry from Irish communities everywhere, and Parks Canada ended up having public hearings right across the country. The creation of Grosse Île as a National Historic Site evoked more interest than any other park in Canada.

By 2005, membership of Irish Heritage Society was over 200; it was collecting artefacts and archives and had a speakers' series. St. Patrick's Day is still observed in Quebec City, with High Mass celebrated at the church, but the annual parade with its arches and marching bands are a thing of the past. Although the Chien d'Or now sells paintings instead of beer, other pubs with an Irish clientele "make something special of the day by having musicians even at breakfast, and the custom of serving green beer," said Marianna O'Gallagher. It's a far cry from the old St. Patrick's Day parades, though. "Some of the waiters dye their hair green and paint shamrocks on their faces," she added balefully, "which doesn't even have the dignity of paganism."

The *Jeanie Johnston*, recreation of an Irish immigrant ship, arriving in Quebec City, September 24, 2003.

The *Jeanie Johnston* was a three-masted sailing ship originally built in Quebec in 1847 by Scottish-born shipbuilder John Munn and pressed into service to carry immigrants from Ireland to North America. This replica was built in Tralee, Ireland. In 2003 it sailed up the St. Lawrence River, stopped at Grosse Île and docked in the Bassin Louise. With the help of Irish Heritage Quebec, Irish Quebecers were able to visit it and better grasp the conditions in which their ancestors travelled on their 40- to 50-day passage from Ireland.

Celtic Cross, Parc de l'Artillerie.

The bond between Irish Quebecers and their ancestral homeland is intense.
This Celtic cross of Irish blue limestone was raised in 2000, and is inscribed
in Gaelic, French and English. It was given by James Callery, descendant
of an Irish famine orphan and director of the Famine Museum in Strokestown,
Ireland. In 1847, a landowner of Strokestown was killed by angry passengers
for hiring unseaworthy ships for emigrants. Music groups such as Rosheen,
the popularity of the Shannon Irish Dancers, the Violon Vert Celtic dance
school and the Saint-Patrick pub attest to the keen attraction of all Quebecers
to all things Celtic.

78th Fraser Highlanders.

The Fraser Highlanders who sunk their Scottish roots in Quebec City in
1759 began putting forth new shoots in this century. A historical garrison
of Fraser Highlanders, Fort St. Andrew's, was founded in 2001, and by 2005
had attracted 40 members. Older members teach the younger to fire their
Brown Bess muskets, dance the sword dance, play the bagpipes and drums
and speak Gaelic. Bagpipe lessons at St. Andrew's Presbyterian Church,
their spiritual home, are open to the public. Together they celebrate Robert
Burns Night, St. Andrew's Day and Tartan Day.

Military honours for American dead.

The American Colony of Quebec was formed in 1944 in response to three American airmen who strayed into Canada and crashed at Saint-Charles-de-Bellechasse near Quebec City. They are buried at Mount Hermon Cemetery, and members still gather there on Memorial Day to honour them. Here a Canadian bugler plays the Last Post. Americans were particularly attracted to Quebec City in the 1960s, and many married francophones and stayed. Early in the 21st century a new wave of Americans began buying property in the Old City, where the "olde worlde" charm and the house prices tempt them to purchase second or third homes.

Dancers from the Beijing Circus, Chinese Festival, Quebec City, 2001.

At the turn of the millennium only about 300 families remained of Quebec City's Chinese community, but in 2001 they asserted their continuing presence by holding the first annual Chinese cultural festival, including dance, martial arts demonstrations and dragon boat races on the St. Charles River. Visitors flocked to Parc de la Jeunesse to see the musicians, acrobats and dancers of the Beijing Chinese Circus, and 20 teams competed in the dragon boat races.

Reading the signs

Choices for the future

Anglophones are becoming more vocal about their forgotten contribution to Quebec City's history, and the city acknowledged some of this contribution in 2000 by renaming Rue Saint-Stanislas "Chaussée des Écossais" (Scots' Way) and erecting an Irish Celtic Cross near the old St. Patrick's Church. But signs have always been contentious in Quebec. With municipal mergers in 2002, many streets of the newly merged city bore identical names, and a renaming of streets was undertaken. Proposals for some historic anglophone names, however, were met with scorn and derision at a public meeting. With its customary discretion, the local English newspaper buried the incident at the end of an article deep in the paper. Discretion as the preferred *modus operandi* was not limited to the newspaper: until 2004 the Literary and Historical Society, the only English library in Quebec City, had no sign to indicate its presence except a piece of paper stuck in the window.

"Before I came here I wasn't aware of the how deep this community's roots are," said Tim Belford, host of the CBC radio morning show since 1993. "Anglophones here are very low-key, but they are also equally at ease in one linguistic community as in the other. They are the best integrated of all anglophones in the province." Fortunately, because entertainment exclusively in English in Quebec is limited. Only a handful of films are shown in English, and even this was achieved only after intense lobbying.

Life for anglophones has changed in Quebec City since the 1980s in other ways too. Although they'll usually be taken for tourists, few anglophones feel ashamed to speak their own language in the street any more. As student Kathleen Stavert said,

> Since we're a minority, we want to show who we are and that we speak English. It's part of our culture, and the francophones are like that too, they're really strong about their French culture. I greatly respect that and I think francophones respect that for the English-speaking people. I don't think the Carnaval or Saint-Jean-Baptiste are just for others: they're for me too. I'm Québécoise and I am part of the Québécois culture. I'd like us to be one big community, with two different families in it.

But with a high rate of intermarriage between anglophones and francophones in Quebec City, assimilation is a distinct possibility. "My father had 12 brothers and sisters," said Richard Walling, executive director of the Holland Centre. "Half of my cousins don't speak English at all." Even children whose mother tongue is English spend their days in French daycare, as most English-speaking mothers are now working. Karen Macdonald has similar observations:

> I speak to my children only in English, but their French is much better than their English. I have friends whose children went to English school and spoke English at home, but now don't speak English at all. In Quebec City, which is such a French environment, the language can be easily lost in one generation. The English-speaking community in Quebec [City] is in the process of assimilation, but we aren't allowed to talk about it, it's not politically correct – there are so many anglophones in Canada, how can it be a problem? But for some places like the Gaspé, Lac Saint-Jean and Quebec City, it's a reality.

What are the choices for the future of the English-speaking communities of Quebec City? Will they assimilate and gradually disappear? Are the government grants that currently sustain many English-speaking institutions and buildings in Quebec City just a stopgap measure, a life-support system that is prolonging their inevitable demise? Will they take refuge in their various ethnic identities and lose any remnants of a shared culture? After all, can eastern European Jewish, Greek Orthodox, Scottish Protestant, Chinese Confucian and Irish Catholic immigrants possibly have anything in common?

They have shared a history in Quebec City, a language, the culturally fruitful experience of being a minority (recently a largely invisible one), strong participation in civil society, an ability to live in several languages, and a desire to share their future with the French-speaking majority. And so the answer to the question of whether Quebec City's diverse English-speaking population can form a community is, extraordinarily, yes.

**Woodcarving by Scott Kingsland
at Atelier Paré Scott.**

Scott Kingsland is one of the many anglophone
artists and craftspeople who have settled
in the Quebec City region. Kingsland and his
wife, Françoise Lavoie, apprenticed to Quebec
master wood sculptor Alphonse Paré, and in
1986 took over his workshop in Sainte-Anne-
de-Beaupré. This economuseum (a Quebec
combination of museum, craft workshop and
store) recounts Quebec legends through wood
sculpture.

**Mural on Bibliothèque Gabrielle Roy showing *Quebec Chronicle-
Telegraph* and its ancestor, the *Quebec Gazette*. © Murale Création**

The wave of murals that has swept over the city began in 1999 when
a French and Québécois mural-painting team completed the vast *La Fresque
des Québécois* beside Côte de la Montagne. Soon after, a band of reformed
graffiti artists transformed the ugly pillars of the Dufferin-Montmorency
overpass into works of art. This 2003 mural on the city library, celebrating
Quebec's literary giants, includes British author Rudyard Kipling, Quebec
historian James MacPherson Le Moine, and the city's first newspaper,
the *Quebec Gazette*, founded by William Brown and Thomas Gilmore
in 1764. It also portrays its living descendant, the *Quebec Chronicle-
Telegraph*.

Calèche.

What goes clip-clop ... bang-bang ... clip-clop?
A drive-by shooting in Vieux-Québec. You may
have trouble finding a book, a film or even a joke
in English in Quebec City, but you can still
always get a tour of the city in English
with Russel Doyle, owner of Les Calèches
du Vieux-Québec for over a quarter of a century.

Children on first day of new Everest Elementary School, 2003.

A 7% jump in enrolment in the Central Quebec School Board in 2002
resulted in the opening of a new English school, Everest Elementary,
the following year. Yet the anglophone population declined by 14% between
1991 and 2001. Perhaps the explanation lies in love: Unilingual Quebec
produces bilingual anglophones who fall in love in French – but send their
children to school in English. In one generation the percentage of Quebec
anglophones with francophone partners has jumped from 20% to over 40%.
The population is busy assimilating, and expanding the pool of children
who inherit access to the English system.

Branching my ordinator

Gallicisms in Quebec City English

In a legendary conversation between two Quebec City writers, Clive Meredith and Marianna O'Gallagher, one of them is said to have replied to the other's question, "I can't answer that because I haven't branched my ordinator yet this morning" (*brancher* means "to plug in" and *ordinateur* means "computer").

"With increasing contact between the two languages," notes the *Oxford Guide to Canadian English Usage*, "more and more French words – particularly those connected to provincial institutions, linguistic politics, and local life – have been assimilated into English, resulting in a new Canadian regional dialect: Quebec English."

Contrary to the conventional attitude to anglicisms in French, where people tend to be "dénoncés pour avoir commis un anglicisme" (denounced for committing an anglicism), Quebec anglophones' reactions to these borrowings are "relatively mild, occasionally rueful, vaguely apologetic and a source of humorous comment rather than a vehement denunciation," according to one researcher. Members of the Laudable Association of Anti-Gallicans, which in the eighteenth century vowed to fight gallicisms in the English language (see Vol. 1 p. 13), must be turning in their graves.

Words that entered Canadian English from Quebec French:

anglophone
cegep
concession
eh? ("hein" & "eh bien")
francophone
mushing
perspective
portage
sovereignty-association
tuque
voyageur
métis

Common gallic constructions in Quebec City English:

accept to meet him
take a decision
I've been here since three days
I go to Quebec High, there
(equivalent of French là)

Direct borrowings of French words (gallicisms) in Quebec City English:

allophone (someone whose first language is neither French or English)
autoroute (highway)
ameliorate (improve)
boite à chanson (nightclub)
caisse [populaire] (bank)
collectivity
congé (holiday)
coureur de bois
de souche
dépanneur (corner store)
fleur-de-lis
flyé (wild)
independentist
joual (slang)
kétaine (kitsch)
péquiste
planification
pure laine (old stock French Quebecers)
rang (concession road)
réveillon (New Year's party)
scolarity (schooling)
subvention (grant)

Faux amis or "false friends" (words that exist in English but are used in Quebec with their French meaning):

animator (group leader)
collaboration (cooperation)
conference (lecture)
confessional (denominational, as in school boards)
coordinates (someone's name and addresses)
delay (deadline, time limit)
demand (ask for something)
determinant (decisive)
formation (training)
formula (form)
global (comprehensive)
inscribe (register)
permanence (tenure, permanent employment)
primordial (essential)
professor (teacher)
recuperate (salvage, recycle)
remark (notice)
resume (summarize)
security (safety)
souvenir (memory)
sympathetic (nice)
vacant (vacancy)

Chronology

1850–1918

1850 Irish orphan Mary Keogh and domestic servant Marie Fitzbach open the Magdalen Asylum for the rehabilitation of women released from prison.

1852 St. Patrick's Literary Institute founded.

Canadian parliament moves from Toronto to Quebec until 1856, and then back to Toronto.

1853 Opening of Chalmers Wesley Church; riot when Gavazzi, a Protestant convert, attacks Roman Catholic Church.

1856 St. Brigid's Asylum opens.

1857 Ottawa chosen as Canadian capital.

1858 Royal Canadians, or 100th Regiment, founded to help put down Indian Mutiny for the British army.

1859 Founding of Ladies' Protestant Home and Irish Protestant Benevolent Society.

Riot at St. Matthew's Anglican Church over church elections.

1860 Canadian parliament moves from Toronto back to Quebec until 1865, and then to Ottawa.

1862 Founding of Quebec Ship Laborers' Benevolent Society.

Founding of Royal Rifles Regiment.

1864 113 vessels built in Quebec City.

1865 Porte Saint-Jean is torn down, followed by the other city gates.

1866 Fenians attempt to invade Canada. Quebec under arms.

1867 British North America Act. Dominion of Canada proclaimed in Quebec City, which becomes capital of new province of Quebec. The Act enshrines educational rights and privileges for Catholics and Protestants. French and English are both official languages. English speakers are now called "Canadians" too.

1871 British regiments leave, removing 3,000 anglophones from city population.

Lord Dufferin begins his "improvements."

The Uniform Currency Act establishes Canadian currency as the only legal tender. British coins are no longer valid, except the gold sovereign, set at $5.

1874 First golf club in Quebec City.

1876 The telephone invented (introduced in Quebec City 1878).

Quebec-Halifax Intercolonial Railway completed.

1879 Quebec, Montreal, Ottawa and Occidental Railway completed.

Pitched battle between French-Canadian and Irish ship labourers in Champlain district.

1880 Garrison Club incorporated. Military men join free, civilians pay fee.

Quebec City is site of first performance of "O Canada," written by Calixa Lavallée and Judge Adolphe Routhier.

1884 St. Patrick's School opens on McMahon Street.

1885 Legislative Assembly adopts Manufacturers' Law which limits work hours to 60 hours a week for women and children, 72.5 hours for men. Employers manage to find loopholes.

1885	Métis Rebellion is put down and Louis Riel is hanged. Public anger fuels French-Canadian Catholic nationalism.
1888	Royal Commission on the Relations between Labor and Capital.
1892	Château Frontenac built.
1896	Wilfrid Laurier abolishes French separate schools in Manitoba.
1897	First car in Quebec City travels at 29 km/h in third gear down Sainte-Foy Road.
	First long-distance hydro line.
1899	Boer War. First Canadian contingent leaves from Quebec. When Henri Bourassa protests against Canadian involvement, he is told to "speak white!"
1900	5,000 shoe workers go on strike for two months.
1901	Death of Queen Victoria.
1902	Quebec Symphony Orchestra founded.
1903	Head tax on Chinese immigrants raised to $500.
1906	Maurice Pollack, a Russian Jewish immigrant, opens a clothing store on St. Joseph Street.
1907	First public assistance act.
	Children under 14 no longer allowed to work.
	Quebec Bridge falls.
1908	Quebec tercentenary celebrations.
1909	Ancient Order of Hibernians raises Celtic Cross at Grosse Île.
1912	Quebec Bulldogs hockey team wins championship of the world.
1913	Ortenberg-Plamondon anti-Semitic libel case tried in Quebec City.
1914	*Empress of Ireland* sinks in the St. Lawrence, drowning 1,024 people.
	World War I breaks out. Quebec City involved in many war-related activities, including munitions and shipbuilding, American ammunition and French shipbuilding bases, and the Yugoslav Mobilization Camp at Lake St. Joseph. Three of the six generals of the Canadian Expeditionary Forces are from Quebec City: Sir Richard Turner, Sir Henry Burstall and Sir David Watson.
1916	Quebec Bridge falls again.
	YWCA opens Douglas Hall gym and swimming pool.
1917	British suffragette Emmeline Pankhurst speaks at Morrin College.
1918	Conscription riots: 4 dead, 70 injured. Martial law proclaimed.
	End of World War I. In Quebec as elsewhere, Spanish flu kills more people than war did.

1919–1976

1921	Quebec nationalizes sale of alcohol.
1923	Chinese excluded from immigrating.
1925	3,000 shoe workers strike against a 30% pay reduction.
1928	Anglo-Canadian Pulp & Paper Mill opens in Hedleyville (Limoilou).
	875,000 tourists visit Quebec City.
	Commission d'Urbanisme changes English street names to French.
1930	William Wood and the Literary and Historical Society suggest the preservation of all buildings within the walled city.
1931	Quebec City's population has doubled since 1901.
1936	New Duplessis government institutes the Padlock Law; police padlock buildings of "Communist sympathizers."
1943	Public schooling compulsory to age 14.
	Quebec Conference: Churchill, Roosevelt and Mackenzie King meet in Quebec City.
1944	Canada adopts conscription; Quebec City MP Chubby Power resigns from the cabinet in protest.
	Quebec women vote in provincial elections for the first time.
1946	Citizens of Canada are now officially "Canadians" instead of British subjects.
1947	Ban on Chinese immigration lifted.
1951	New Jeffery Hale Hospital built.
1957	CKMI, Quebec City's English TV station, goes on air.
1958	St. Lawrence College opens.
1959	Maurice Duplessis dies.
1960	Jean Lesage's Liberals are elected; beginning of the Quiet Revolution.
1964	Bill 60 creates Quebec's first Ministry of Education.
	Queen Elizabeth II visits Quebec City; remembered as "Nightstick Saturday" (*samedi de la matraque*) because of police brutality towards protesters.
1965	First Jewish commissioner, Isidore C. Pollack, elected to Protestant School Board.
1967	Visit to Quebec City of French President Charles de Gaulle, who then proceeds upriver to Montreal and delivers his famous "Vive le Québec Libre" speech.
1968	Quebec's Legislative Assembly renamed the National Assembly.
	Gendron Commission on language. Commissioners booed and attacked by students at CEGEP Sainte-Foy.
1969	1,239 buildings demolished, including the old Irish district, for Cité Parlementaire.
	Bill 63: 30,000 demonstrate in front of Parliament against language choice in education.
1970	October Crisis: kidnapping of James Cross (British trade commissioner in Montreal) and murder of Pierre Laporte (Minister of Labour) by Front de Libération du Québec.
1971	About half the Quebec City region's British-origin population now speak French as their mother tongue.
1974	Bill 22 recognizes French as official language of Quebec and restricts access to English schools to "children with sufficient knowledge of English."
1975	CRTC shuts down CFOM, Quebec City's bilingual pop radio station.
1976	Parti Québécois, dedicated to taking Quebec out of Confederation, comes to power.
	Citadel Foundation is founded with funds from High School of Quebec and other defunct anglophone institutions.

Since 1976

1977 First English-language rights group forms in Quebec City, predecessor of Voice of English Quebec (VEQ), founded in 1981.

Charte de la langue française (Bill 101) makes Quebec unilingually French. Only children with a parent educated in English in Quebec can go to English schools.

1978 Cullen-Couture Accord brings more Quebec immigrants from French-speaking countries.

1979 CBC radio opens station in Quebec City.

Quebec Chronicle-Telegraph saved from ignominious demise.

1980 59.5% of Quebecers vote against sovereignty in referendum. In Quebec City, 48% say Yes.

1982 Canadian constitution patriated without Quebec's signature.

Canadian Charter of Rights and Freedoms includes "Canada Clause": anyone educated in English in *Canada* (not just Quebec) can send their children to English school in Quebec.

1985 Parti Québécois defeated by Robert Bourassa's Liberals.

1986 Bill 142 gives Quebecers right to limited health and social services in English.

1988 Bill 178 mandates French signs only. As Supreme Court rules it violates Canadian Charter of Rights and Freedoms, Premier Robert Bourassa invokes notwithstanding clause. At a public meeting VEQ accuses government of "using the notwithstanding clause against the anglophone minority of Quebec."

1989 Ladies' Protestant Home closes.

1990 Holland Centre opens, offering English language health and social services.

Meech Lake Constitutional Accord, supported by VEQ and a majority of Quebec City anglophones, dies when two provinces fail to ratify it.

1992 Defeat of Charlottetown Accord, also supported by VEQ.

1993 Notwithstanding Clause runs out for Bill 178. Bill 86 allows bilingual signs, but French must be bigger. Existing bilingual public services are maintained.

1994 Parti Québécois elected again under Jacques Parizeau.

1995 In 2nd referendum, narrow majority against sovereignty. Premier Parizeau's use of pronoun "we" plays into fears about real goals of sovereigntists. Parizeau resigns and is succeeded by Lucien Bouchard.

1998 Catholic and Protestant (denominational) school boards replaced by English and French (linguistic) school boards.

2001 Premier Bouchard resigns in midst of controversy sparked by PQ candidate Yves Michaud's remarks about Jews obstructing sovereignty.

1.5% of Quebec City region's total population is anglophone. Ninety per cent of the anglophones know French.

Regiment of Fraser Highlanders, Fort St. Andrew's Garrison, founded in Quebec City.

2002 Restructured health boards threaten to subsume anglophone services. After three years of negotiations the Jeffery Hale Hospital, St. Brigid's Home and the Holland Centre fuse into one institution with a specific mandate for the region's anglophones.

2003 PQ defeated by Liberals under Jean Charest.

2004 Opening of Everest Elementary, new anglophone public school.

2005 Morrin College converted into Morrin Centre, a cultural interpretation centre for the anglophone community.

Further Reading

There has been very little published on anglophones of Quebec City over the past century, and I only hope this book will be a launching pad for in-depth research on the many topics that I have only been able to treat in a cursory fashion.

1850–1918

Information specific to Quebec City anglophones peters out during this period, but can be found in various focused works, such as H.V. Nelles's *The Art of Nation-Building: Pageantry and Spectacle at Quebec's Tercentenary* (Toronto: University of Toronto Press, 1999), which gives a good overview of life in Quebec City in 1908. The books of Marianna O'Gallagher are important resources on the Irish of Quebec City (Grosse Île, St. Brigid's Home and St. Patrick's Parish), as is Robert Grace's indispensable *The Irish in Quebec: An Introduction to the Historiography* (Quebec: Institut québécois de recherche sur la culture, 1993). Ronald Rudin's *The Forgotten Quebecers: A History of English-Speaking Quebec, 1759–1980* (Quebec: Institut québécois de recherche sur la culture, 1985) is also essential reading for this and other periods, especially on demographics and education.

1918–1976

No books have been written on Quebec City anglophones of this period. Overviews of anglophones in Quebec province can be found in *The English of Quebec: From Majority to Minority*, edited by Gary Caldwell and Eric Waddell (Quebec: Institut québécois de recherche sur la culture, 1982), and *A Short History of Quebec* by Brian Young and John A. Dickinson (Montreal: McGill-Queen's University Press, 2003). See also Serge Courville and Robert Garon's *Atlas historique du Québec, ville et capitale* (Sainte-Foy: Archives nationales du Québec, 2001).

Since 1976

There is plenty to read on Quebec's Quiet Revolution, referenda and language legislation, depending on your politics. On the one hand there is Josée Legault's *L'invention d'une minorité: les Anglo-Québécois* (Montreal: Boréal, 1992), and on the other there is Reed Scowen's *Time to Say Goodbye: The Case for Getting Quebec Out of Canada* (Toronto: McClelland & Stewart, 1999). Garth Stevenson takes the reader painstakingly through the "language and nation" events of the 1970s and 1980s in his *Community Besieged: The Anglophone Minority and the Politics of Quebec* (Montreal: McGill-Queens 1999). None of these look at the specific (and distinct) situation of Quebec City.

Index

Illustration Credits

Chapter 1
Page

2 – Library and Archives Canada, e000996429
4 – Library and Archives Canada, C-150009
5 – Bibliothèque nationale du Québec
5 – Literary and Historical Society of Quebec
7 – Archives nationales du Québec in Quebec City
8 – Art Gallery of Ontario
8 – Library and Archives Canada, C-150278
9 – Musée national des beaux-arts du Québec
10 – Library and Archives Canada, C-150717
11 – Bibliothèque nationale du Québec
12 – Archives de l'Archidiocèse de Québec
13 – Archives de l'Archidiocèse de Québec
13 – Jane Wong collection
14 – Jules Goodman collection
14 – Library and Archives Canada, PA-010400
15 – Jacques Saint-Pierre collection
16 – Jacques Saint-Pierre collection
17 – Musée national des beaux-arts du Québec
17 – Jacques Saint-Pierre collection
18 – McCord Museum
19 – McCord Museum, I-76319
20 – Bibliothèque nationale du Québec
21 – Archives de la Ville de Québec
22 – Musée national des beaux-arts du Québec
23 – Archives de la Ville de Québec
23 – Museum of London, U.K.

Chapter 2
Page

24 – Musée national des beaux-arts du Québec
26 – Library and Archives Canada, C-042292
27 – Barbara Bignell collection
28 – Yves Beauregard collection

29 – Luc-Antoine Couturier
29 – Bibliothèque nationale du Québec
29 – Library and Archives Canada, e003525477
31 – Schmidt, Nancy, *Irish for a Day: Saint Patrick's Day Celebrations in Quebec City, 1765–1990*. Quebec City: Carraig Books, 1991.
31 – Blair Family collection
31 – Library and Archives Canada, C-084469
32 – Bibliothèque nationale du Québec
32 – Archives nationales du Québec in Quebec City
33 – Jeffery Hale Hospital
34 – McCord Museum
34 – Bibliothèque nationale du Québec
35 – Les Photographes Kedl
36 – Literary and Historical Society of Quebec
37 – Archives nationales du Québec in Quebec City
37 – Yves Beauregard collection
39 – Musée de la civilisation, 1991.173

Chapter 3
Page

40 – Art Gallery of Ontario
42 – Musée de la civilisation, 1993.15879
43 – National Battlefields Commission
43 – Royal 22nd Regiment Museum
44 – Archives nationales du Québec in Quebec City
45 – Archives nationales du Québec in Quebec City
46 – Library and Archives Canada, C-121142
47 – Archives de la Ville de Québec and Archives nationales du Québec in Quebec City
48 – Boswell Family collection
49 – Boswell Family collection
49 – Yves Beauregard collection
49 – Bibliothèque nationale du Québec
50 – Archives nationales du Québec in Quebec City
51 – Archives nationales du Québec in Quebec City

Chapter 4

Page

Chapter 5

Page